Quilt in a Day®

Kaleidoscope Quilt

Eleanor Burns

For Mother and Father...

You put the "sparkle" in my life.

Copyright 1996 Eleanor A. Burns Family Trust

ISBN 0-922795-49-6

First Printing February 1996

Art Direction Merritt Voigtlander
Graphic Artist Susan Sells

Published by Quilt in a Day®, Inc. 1955 Diamond Street, San Marcos, CA 92069

Table of Contents

Introduction

Optical toys were very popular during the Victorian Era, as parlor games and as educational toys. Families gathered round to marvel at devices such as the "Magic Lantern," the stereoscope, and the kaleidoscope. Early kaleidoscopes were finely crafted, expensive, ornamental items.

Over the years, the kaleidoscope has become one of childhood's enduring favorites. Did you have one? I could spend hours peering through my kaleidoscope, fascinated by the endlessly changing patterns, experimenting to see how the light changed the colors as I pointed it toward a sunny window or the shade of a tree.

Maybe that's why I found the Kaleidoscope quilt pattern so captivating! As the colorful pieces fall together in a variety of intricate designs, I can imagine I'm looking through my childhood kaleidoscope. Patterns for the Kaleidoscope block can be traced to the early 1930's. Capper's Weekly, a farm journal, first published a version in 1930. The Kansas City Star newspaper, which began a column of traditional and new designs in the early thirties, published many variations of this block, with such picturesque names as Golden Wedding Quilt, Massachusetts Priscilla, and Sugar Cone. The Kaleidoscope also appeared in the women's publication Workbasket in 1935.

As I've worked on my Kaleidoscope quilts, observing how patterns emerge from the dark and light hues of the fabric, it's come to me how life is like an old-time kaleidoscope toy… and how my family tumbles into the concentric design as their favorite colors. Mother and Father are the central blue pieces of glass, for they created the feeling of safety within the family unit. Grant and I share that same true blue - pieces that sooth our nerves and souls. Judy's blue pieces of contemplation sparkle with a touch of purple. On the fringe of these blue crystals are complimenting diamonds… Kathy's in peach for social energy, and Patricia's in pink for universal love. Sprinkled throughout the blues and pastels of the family unit are Orion's yellow stars for joy.

Around the edges, my brother Bruce's family explodes and sparkles as green… green for youth and prosperity, green for nature, spring, and protecting the environment.

Colorful pieces fall together just as the events of our lives transpire, shifting scenes and changing patterns, never repeating.

May the colorful pieces of this quilt brighten your life!

Eleanor Burns

About the Quilt

The basic unit of a Kaleidoscope quilt is a square block divided into eight large triangles radiating from a center and finished with small triangles added to the four corners.

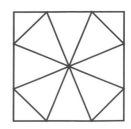

A careful arrangement of these simple large and small triangles can fool the eye into seeing large circles despite the fact that the Kaleidoscope quilt has no curved lines.

Because the center of the block and sides have many points to match, the Kaleidoscope quilt should only be made by quiltmakers with experience.

When nine blocks are sewn together into a square with color, a Star emerges from the Center. A Background interlocking circle surrounds the Star.

The Star is made of eight large triangles cut from strips 5" wide. ■

The Star Center is made of four large triangles cut from strips 5" wide. ■

The Background surrounding the Star is made of large triangles cut from strips 5" wide and small triangles cut from strips 4" wide. ☐

Once additional uneven numbers of blocks are sewn together, the eye starts moving across the pattern, roving from circles to Stars, losing touch with the basic unit.

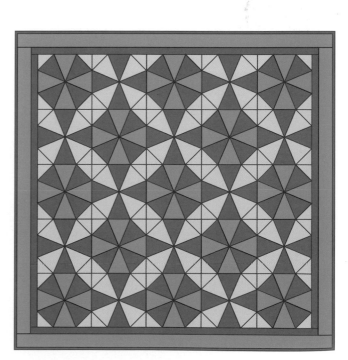

Two Different Kaleidoscope Designs

Two Kaleidoscope designs are given for different looks. Choose one of these:

- Overall Pattern
- Edge Block Pattern

The Overall Pattern

The Overall Pattern is constructed from two colorations of the basic block.
Blocks are arranged in alternating order.
More of the pattern can be seen, particularly in the smaller quilts.
However, outside points do not appear on the outer stars.

①Star / Center Block

②Star / Background Block

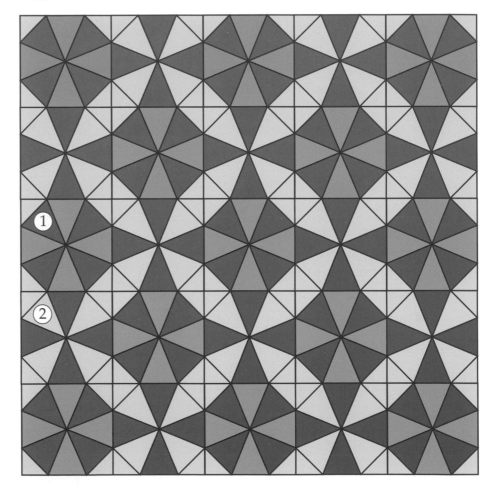

An option for the pattern is to applique points onto the border strip in order to complete the outer stars. See page 81.

The Edge Block Pattern

The Pattern with Edge Blocks is constructed from five colorations of the basic block. The outside edge makes this pattern unique. The Background frames the Stars, clearly defining each one, and outside Stars in the Edge Blocks are complete.

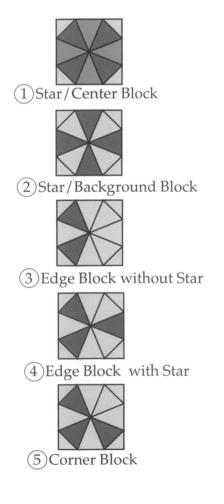

1 Star / Center Block

2 Star / Background Block

3 Edge Block without Star

4 Edge Block with Star

5 Corner Block

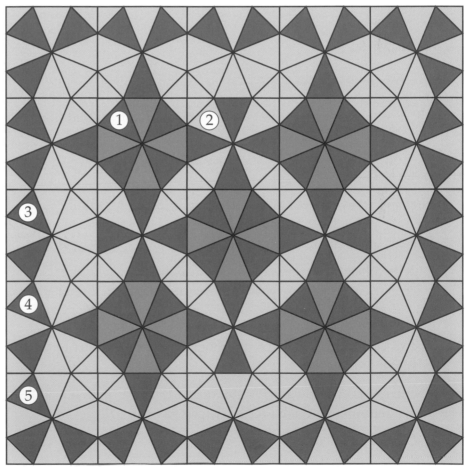

If you are making your quilt with the Edge Block Pattern, the instructions for blocks 3, 4 and 5 are highlighted with the block pattern on the side of the pages.

Fabric Selection and Values

Fabric and Thread Selection

Use all 100% cotton fabrics **of same weight** for your Kaleidoscope quilt. Do not use blends or heavy decorator fabrics. Use a gray or slightly contrasting color of thread, so seams and match points are easily seen.

Values of Fabric

Value placement of lights, mediums, and darks in the Kaleidoscope block are extremely important. In the finished quilt, the viewer's eye travels from circle to circle, star to star, or perhaps to the points, each time discovering a new element within the quilt. When a value is randomly placed, the pattern becomes distorted and moves the eye in a new direction.

Two sets of yardage charts are given for both Overall and Edge Block patterns. Select one of these:

- **Three Fabric Blocks or**
- **Multi-Fabric Blocks**

Three Fabric Blocks

Select three fabrics in different values, generally light for Background, medium for Star Center, and dark for Star. It is important to have contrast between the Star and Background. Mix the scales of your prints, as small, medium, and large scale prints, or prints that read solid from a distance, or small checks.

Multi-Fabric Blocks

Gather and sort your stash of fabric into piles of light, medium and dark values. Once you have them sorted, stand back and squint at the values. Change any that stand out. Viewing the fabric through a Ruby Beholder™ also helps distinguish values.

Each strip called for in the yardage chart can be a different one. For variety, use half and quarter strips, but provide extra strips because you get fewer triangles from shorter strips.

Background

- The same fabric can be used throughout the quilt. Refer to the Background yardage listed under Three Fabric Blocks.
- Quarter yard pieces and "fat quarters" (18" x 22" pieces) lend themselves well to 4" and 5" strips, the two measurements used for the large and small triangles in the Background.

Star Centers and Stars

- The Star Centers and Stars are large triangles cut from 5" strips.
- A variety of one third yard pieces can be cut into (2) 5" strips, particularly useful for larger quilts.

This "look" was created by using three fabrics in the block.

Background - Circles Surrounding the Stars
- White print on white fabric

Center of Stars
- Medium scale floral print

Star
- Tone-on-tone; reads "solid" from a distance

Additional fabrics were used in the Second Border and Folded Border.

Quilt made by Sue Bouchard

These quilts were made with multiple fabrics. The Center values are different in each one.

Background - Circles Surrounding the Stars
- off-white print on muslin fabric
- sparsely scattered florals on off-white fabric

Center of Stars
- light or light medium floral fabrics

Star
- dark medium or dark floral fabrics

Because the stars are not as well defined, there is more "movement" in the quilt, and is best viewed from a distance.

Overall Pattern by Eleanor Burns

Background - Circles Surrounding the Stars
- off-white print on muslin fabric
- white or off-white with sparsely scattered florals

Center of Stars
- dark medium fabric in floral
- prints that read "solid" from a distance

Star
- dark fabric in floral
- prints that read "solid" from a distance

The dark medium in the centers of each star adds clarity to the design, and there is not as much movement as in the first quilt.

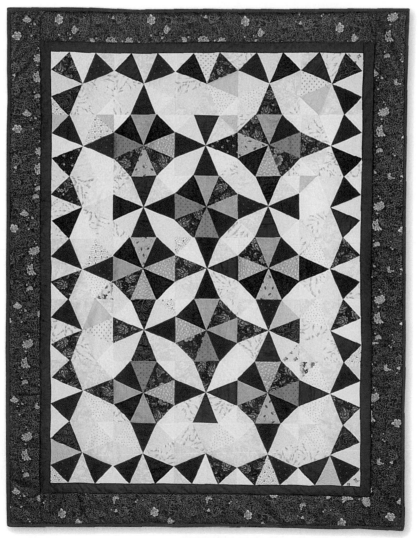

Edge Block Pattern by Eleanor Burns

Supplies

- Wooden Iron

- Gridded pressing mat
- Gridded cutting mat

- Stiletto

- Large rotary cutter
  with new blade

Plexiglass rulers

- 6" x 24" long ruler
- Kaleidoscope Ruler
- 12 ½" Square Up Ruler

For machine quilting

- Invisible thread
- Quilt clips
- Binder clips or masking tape
- Walking foot attachment
- Pinning tool
- 1" Safety pins

- Adhesive Strip for Seam Guide

Plan Your Quilt

You have permission to make photocopies of this page.
Pencil in your design with colored pencils the same colors as your fabrics.
Refer to Yardage Charts on pages 14-25.

Star/Center Block 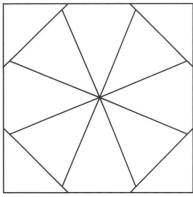 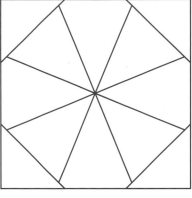 Star/Background Block

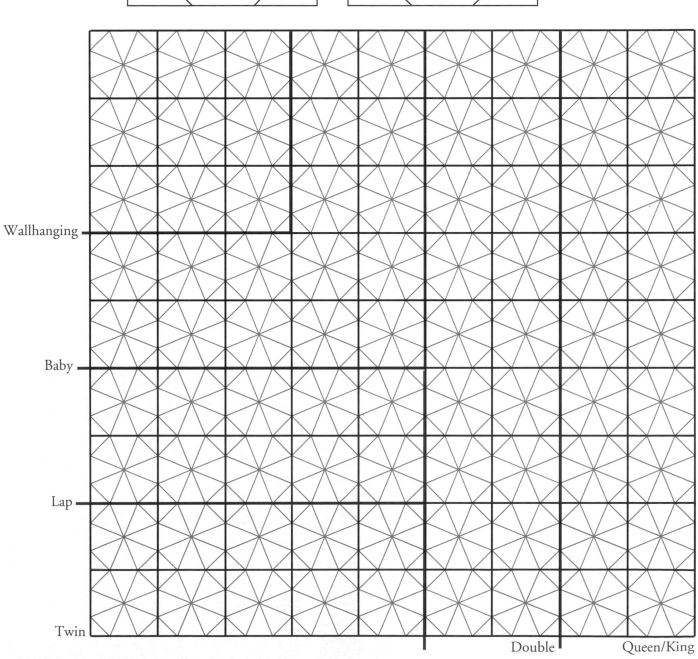

Wallhanging

Baby

Lap

Twin

Double Queen/King

Yardage Charts

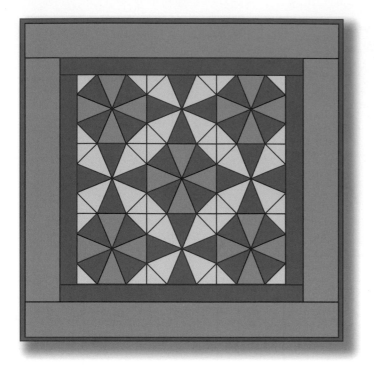

Wallhanging

Overall Pattern
9 Blocks
3 x 3
34" x 34"

THREE FABRIC BLOCKS *Cut into Strips as Listed in Multi-Fabric Column*		MULTI-FABRIC BLOCKS *Cut a Variety of Strips to Total Amounts in this Column*
Background	⅔ yd	(2) 5" x 42" strips (2) 4" x 42" strips Cut into (18) 4" squares; then cut on diagonal
Star Center	⅓ yd	(2) 5" x 42" strips
Star	⅔ yd	(4) 5" x 42" strips
First Border	⅓ yd	(4) 2" x 42" strips
Second Border	⅝ yd	(4) 4" x 42" strips
Backing	1¼ yds	
Batting	40" square	
Binding	½ yd	(4) 3" x 42" strips

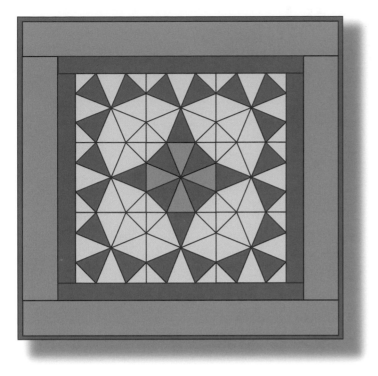

Wallhanging

Edge Block Pattern
9 Blocks
3 x 3
34" x 34"

THREE FABRIC BLOCKS Cut into Strips as Listed in Multi-Fabric Column		MULTI-FABRIC BLOCKS Cut a Variety of Strips to Total Amounts in this Column
Background	1 yd	(4) 5" x 42" strips (2) 4" x 42" strips Cut into (18) 4" squares; then cut on diagonal
Star Center	¼ yd	(1) 5" x 42" strip
Star	½ yd	(3) 5" x 42" strips
First Border	⅓ yd	(4) 2" x 42" strips
Second Border	⅝ yd	(4) 4" x 42" strips
Backing	1¼ yds	
Batting	40" square	
Binding	½ yd	(4) 3" x 42" strips

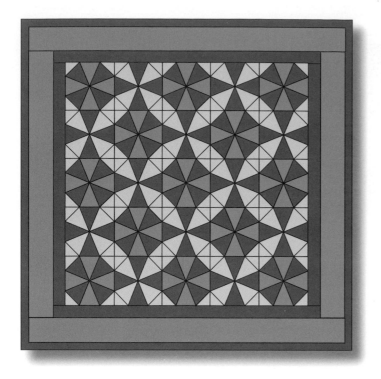

Baby

Overall Pattern
25 Blocks
5 x 5
50" x 50"

THREE FABRIC BLOCKS *Cut into Strips as Listed in Multi-Fabric Column*		MULTI-FABRIC BLOCKS *Cut a Variety of Strips to Total Amounts in this Column*
Background	1¼ yds	(3) 5" x 42" strips (5) 4" x 42" strips Cut into (50) 4" squares; then cut on diagonal
Star Center	⅝ yd	(3) 5" x 42" strips
Star	1 yd	(6) 5" x 42" strips
First Border	⅓ yd	(5) 2" x 42" strips
Second Border	⅔ yd	(5) 4" x 42" strips
Backing	3 yds	Cut 2 equal pieces
Batting	54" square	
Binding	½ yd	(5) 3" x 42" strips

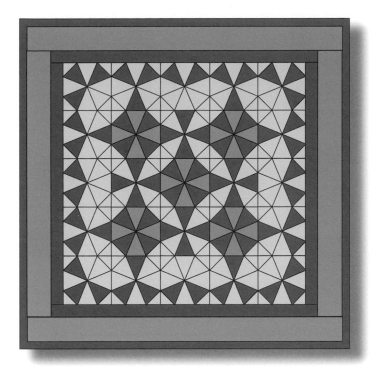

Baby

Edge Block Pattern
25 Blocks
5 x 5
50" x 50"

THREE FABRIC BLOCKS *Cut into Strips as Listed in Multi-Fabric Column*		MULTI-FABRIC BLOCKS *Cut a Variety of Strips to Total Amounts in this Column*
Background	1⅞ yds	(8) 5" x 42" strips (5) 4" x 42" strips Cut into (50) 4" squares; then cut on diagonal
Star Center	⅜ yd	(2) 5" x 42" strips
Star	1¼ yds	(7) 5" x 42" strips
First Border	⅓ yd	(5) 2" x 42" strips
Second Border	⅔ yd	(5) 4" x 42" strips
Backing	3 yds	Cut 2 equal pieces
Batting	54" square	
Binding	½ yd	(5) 3" x 42" strips

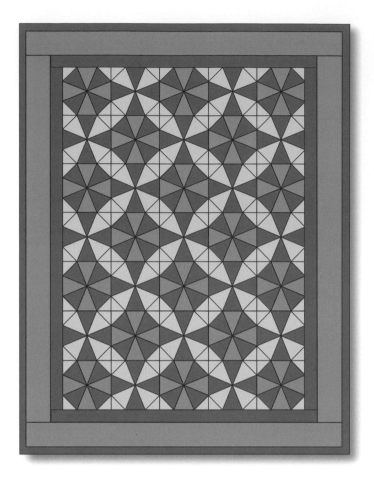

Lap

Overall Pattern
35 Blocks
5 x 7
52" x 68"

THREE FABRIC BLOCKS *Cut into Strips as Listed in Multi-Fabric Column*		MULTI-FABRIC BLOCKS *Cut a Variety of Strips to Total Amounts in this Column*
Background	1½ yds	(4) 5" x 42" strips (7) 4" x 42" strips Cut into (70) 4" squares; then cut on diagonal
Star Center	¾ yd	(4) 5" x 42" strips
Star	1¼ yds	(8) 5" x 42" strips
First Border	½ yd	(5) 2½" x 42"strips
Second Border	1 yd	(6) 4½" x 42" strips
Backing	3⅓ yds	Cut 2 equal pieces
Batting	60" x 72"	
Binding	⅔ yd	(6) 3" x 42" strips

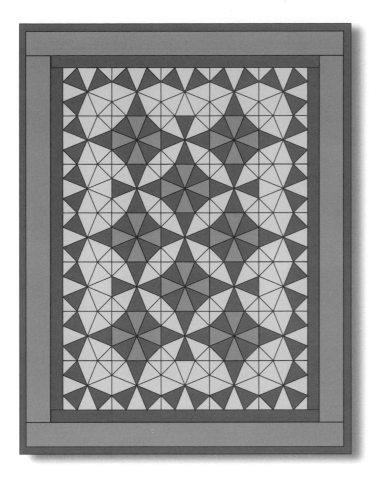

Lap

Edge Block Pattern
35 Blocks
5 x 7
52" x 68"

THREE FABRIC BLOCKS		MULTI-FABRIC BLOCKS	
Cut into Strips as Listed in Multi-Fabric Column		*Cut a Variety of Strips to Total Amounts in this Column*	
Background	2¼ yds	(9) 5" x 42" strips	
		(7) 4" x 42" strips	
		Cut into (70) 4" squares; then cut on diagonal	
Star Center	⅜ yd	(2) 5" x 42" strips	
Star	1¼ yds	(7) 5" x 42" strips	
First Border	½ yd	(5) 2½" x 42" strips	
Second Border	1 yd	(6) 4½" x 42" strips	
Backing	3⅓ yds	Cut 2 equal pieces	
Batting	60" x 72"		
Binding	⅔ yd	(6) 3" x 42" strips	

Twin

Overall Pattern
45 Blocks
5 x 9
65" x 97"

THREE FABRIC BLOCKS *Cut into Strips as Listed in Multi-Fabric Column*		MULTI-FABRIC BLOCKS *Cut a Variety of Strips to Total Amounts in this Column*
Background	2 yds	(6) 5" x 42" strips (9) 4" x 42" strips Cut into (90) 4" squares; then cut on diagonal
Star Center	1 yd	(6) 5" x 42" strips
Star	1⅞ yds	(12) 5" x 42" strips
First Border	⅝ yd	(6) 2½" x 42" strips
Second Border	⅞ yd	(7) 4½" x 42" strips
Third Border	1½ yds	(7) 7" x 42" strips
Backing	6 yds	Cut 2 equal pieces
Batting	72" x 108"	
Binding	¾ yd	(8) 3" x 42" strips

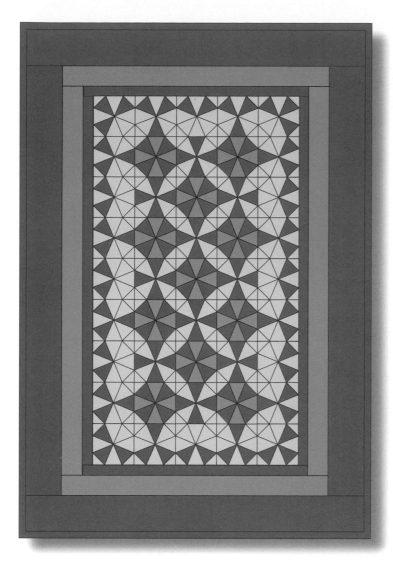

Twin

Edge Block Pattern
45 Blocks
5 x 9
65" x 97"

THREE FABRIC BLOCKS		MULTI-FABRIC BLOCKS	
Cut into Strips as Listed in Multi-Fabric Column		*Cut a Variety of Strips to Total Amounts in this Column*	
Background	2⅔ yds	(11) 5" x 42" strips	
		(9) 4" x 42" strips	
		Cut into (90) 4" squares; then cut on diagonal	
Star Center	⅝ yd	(3) 5" x 42" strips	
Star	1⅝ yds	(10) 5" x 42" strips	
First Border	⅝ yd	(6) 2½" x 42" strips	
Second Border	⅞ yd	(7) 4½" x 42" strips	
Third Border	1½ yds	(7) 7" x 42" strips	
Backing	6 yds	Cut 2 equal pieces	
Batting	72" x 108"		
Binding	¾ yd	(8) 3" x 42" strips	

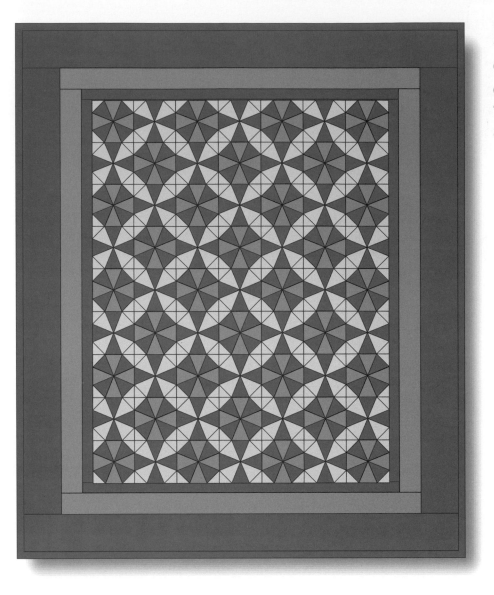

Double

Overall Pattern
63 Blocks
7 x 9
81" x 97"

THREE FABRIC BLOCKS		MULTI-FABRIC BLOCKS	
Cut into Strips as Listed in Multi-Fabric Column		*Cut a Variety of Strips to Total Amounts in this Column*	
Background	2⅝ yds	(7) 5" x 42" strips (13) 4" x 42" strips Cut into (126) 4" squares; then cut on diagonal	
Star Center	1¼ yds	(7) 5" x 42" strips	
Star	2⅛ yds	(14) 5" x 42" strips	
First Border	⅔ yd	(7) 2½" x 42" strips	
Second Border	1 yd	(7) 4½" x 42" strips	
Third Border	2 yds	(9) 7" x 42" strips	
Backing	6 yds	Cut 2 equal pieces	
Batting	86" x 108"		
Binding	1 yd	(9) 3" x 42" strips	

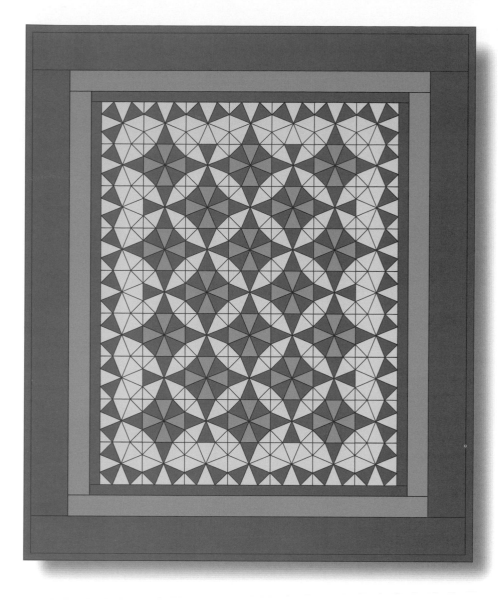

Double

Edge Block Pattern
63 Blocks
7 x 9
81" x 97"

THREE FABRIC BLOCKS *Cut into Strips as Listed in Multi-Fabric Column*		MULTI-FABRIC BLOCKS *Cut a Variety of Strips to Total Amounts in this Column*
Background	3½ yds	(12) 5" x 42" strips (13) 4" x 42" strips Cut into (126) 4" squares; then cut on diagonal
Star Center	¾ yd	(4) 5" x 42" strips
Star	2 yds	(12) 5" x 42" strips
First Border	⅔ yd	(7) 2½" x 42" strips
Second Border	1 yd	(7) 4½" x 42" strips
Third Border	2 yds	(9) 7" x 42" strips
Backing	6 yds	Cut 2 equal pieces
Batting	86" x 108"	
Binding	1 yd	(9) 3" x 42" strips

THREE FABRIC BLOCKS *Cut into Strips as Listed in Multi-Fabric Column*		MULTI-FABRIC BLOCKS *Cut a Variety of Strips to Total Amounts in this Column*
Background	3½ yds	(10) 5" x 42" strips (17) 4" x 42" strips Cut into (162) 4" squares; then cut on diagonal
Star Center	1⅝ yds	(10) 5" x 42" strips
Star	3 yds	(20) 5" x 42" strips
First Border	⅔ yd	(7) 2½" x 42" strips
Second Border	1¼ yds	(8) 4½" x 42" strips
Third Border	2¼ yds	(11) 7" x 42" strips
Backing	9 yds	Cut 3 equal pieces
Batting	120" x 120"	
Binding	1⅛ yds	(12) 3" x 42" strips

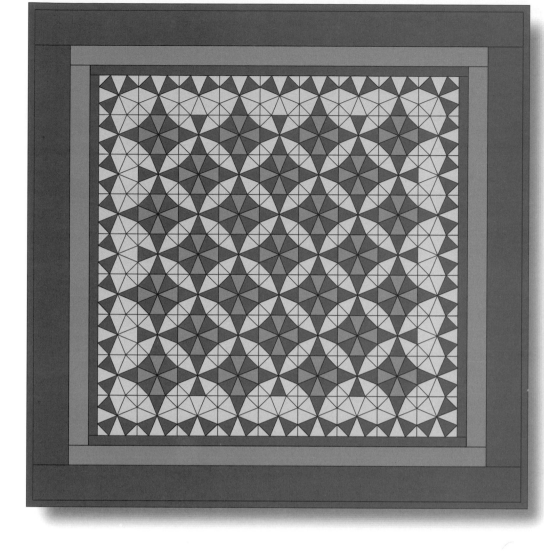

Queen/King

Edge Block Pattern
81 Blocks
9 x 9
97" x 97"

THREE FABRIC BLOCKS		MULTI-FABRIC BLOCKS	
Cut into Strips as Listed in Multi-Fabric Column		*Cut a Variety of Strips to Total Amounts in this Column*	
Background	4⅓ yds	(16) 5" x 42" strips	
		(17) 4" x 42" strips	
		Cut into (162) 4" squares; then cut on diagonal	
Star Center	1 yd	(5) 5" x 42" strips	
Star	2¼ yds	(15) 5" x 42" strips	
First Border	⅔ yd	(7) 2½" x 42" strips	
Second Border	1¼ yds	(8) 4½" x 42" strips	
Third Border	2¼ yds	(11) 7" x 42" strips	
Backing	9 yds	Cut 3 equal pieces	
Batting	120" x 120"		
Binding	1⅛ yds	(12) 3" x 42" strips	

General Cutting and Sewing

Cutting Strips for Large Triangles

Follow your appropriate size chart for specific numbers of strips. The large triangles are from **5" wide strips cut selvage to selvage.**

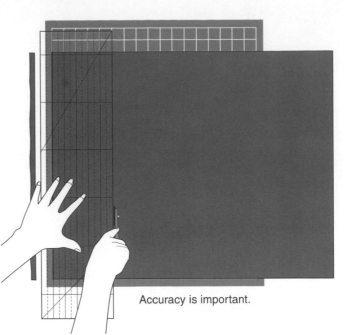

1. Make a nick on the selvage edge, and tear your fabric from selvage to selvage to put the fabric on straight of grain.

2. Fold the fabric in half, matching the torn straight edge thread to thread.

3. With the fold of the fabric at the top, line up the torn edge of fabric on the gridded cutting mat with the left edge extended slightly to the left of zero. Reverse this procedure if you are left-handed.

4. Line up the 6" x 24" ruler on zero. Spread the fingers of your left hand to hold the ruler firmly. With the rotary cutter in your right hand, begin cutting the fabric off with the blade on the mat. Put all your strength into the rotary cutter as you cut away from you, and trim the torn, ragged edge.

Accuracy is important.

5. Lift, and move the ruler over until it lines up with the 5" strip width on the grid and cut.

6. Open the first strip to see if it is straight. Check periodically. Make a straightening cut when necessary.

Multi-Fabrics Blocks

For variety in placement of multiple fabrics, particularly in smaller quilts, cut the 5" strips into two pieces or four pieces. Total your quarter and half strips to equal full strips.

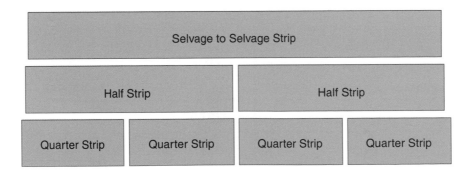

Cutting Strips for Borders

Border strips are also cut selvage to selvage with a 6" x 24" ruler. Follow the appropriate yardage chart for specific measurements and amounts.

Cutting Strips for Small Background Corner Triangles

The small Background triangles are first cut from **4" strips into 4" squares**, and then cut on one diagonal. Follow your appropriate size chart for specific numbers of strips and squares.

1. Cut strips 4" wide from selvage to selvage with the 6" x 24" ruler.

2. Layer cut 4" squares from that strip.

3. Layer cut each square on the diagonal.

4. Place in eight equal stacks.

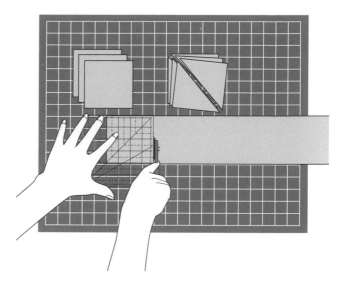

Sewing

Stitch size

Use a small stitch, 15 to the inch or a setting of 2.

¼" seam allowance

Use a consistent ¼" seam allowance throughout construction. A **strip of adhesive** placed at the right of the presser foot will assure a consistent seam allowance. Line up the needle with the ¼" gauge and place the adhesive strip next to it.

Stiletto

Use the **stiletto** to separate pairs of triangles and feed them through the sewing machine, hold the seams flat, and remove the stitches for the "pinwheel" center.

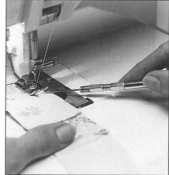

¼" Seam Allowance · Stiletto

Pressing

Gridded Pressing Mat

Use a **gridded pressing mat** to help keep long pieces pressed straight. The cushion allows the thick "pinwheel" center seam on the finished block to "sink in" so the block can be pressed flat.

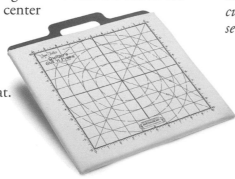

Wooden Iron

Use a **"wooden iron"** for pressing triangle seams to one side. *Pressing with a regular iron distorts the bias cuts on triangles, and makes the blocks difficult to sew together.*

Making the Blocks

 The Star/Center Blocks ①
Layer Cutting Triangles from Sets of Strips

1. Working from the bottom upward, **layer four 5" strips** right sides together in this order:

   *Place a **Star strip** on the **bottom right side up.** Place a Center strip right sides together to the Star. Place a **second Star strip on the stack right side up**, and a **Center strip right sides together** to it. Four selvage to selvage strips are referred to as a Strip Set.*

   If you have more than one fabric for your Star and Center, use a different fabric for each strip. Layer cutting works best with 5" strips cut approximately the same length.

Strip Set

These four strips are layered in pairs right sides together, so, once they are cut into triangles, they are ready for sewing.

2. Carefully line up the edges and left selvage end.

3. Press.

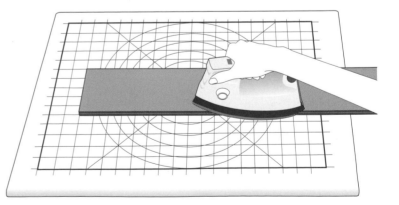

   If you find that your strips will not line up because of "dips" at the center fold, cut the strips in half at the center fold. Proceed with the two half strips. Because you get fewer triangles with half and quarter strips, you may need to cut extra strips.

4. Line up the pressed set of strips with the grid on the cutting mat.

5. Place the triangle ruler on the left end of the strip set. Line up the center of the ruler to the right of the selvage. Line the 5" base line of the ruler with the bottom edge of strip. Check that the perpendicular line on the ruler is parallel with the lines on the grid.

6. Holding the ruler firmly, cut up the right side of the ruler with the rotary cutter, trimming the selvage edges. Remove the selvage end excess.

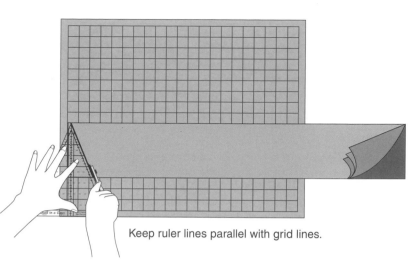

Keep ruler lines parallel with grid lines.

7. Lift up and turn the ruler so that the 5" base line of the ruler lines up exactly with the top of the strip set.

8. Cut again. **Four triangles are in this stack.**

   Each cut, check that lines on ruler are parallel with lines on grid. Make straightening cuts if necessary.

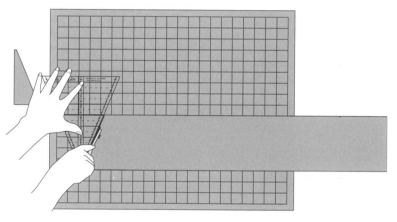

9. Lift up and turn the ruler so that the 5" base line of the ruler lines up exactly with the bottom of the strip set. Cut. **Four triangles are in this stack.**

10. Repeat this cutting process until you have the 5" layered set of strips cut into triangles. Make straightening cuts if necessary.

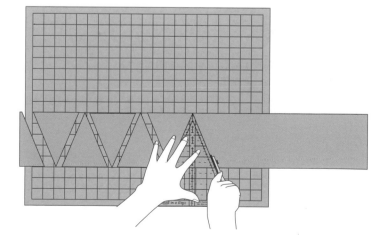

You should get 18-20 stacks of triangles from 4 layered strips cut selvage to selvage.

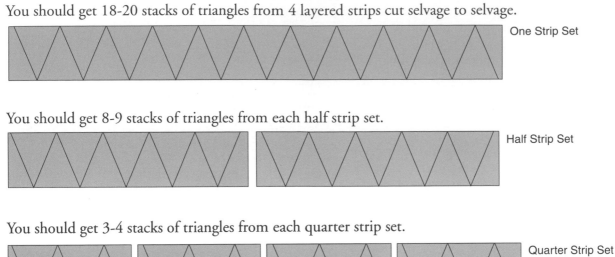

One Strip Set

You should get 8-9 stacks of triangles from each half strip set.

Half Strip Set

You should get 3-4 stacks of triangles from each quarter strip set.

Quarter Strip Set

11. **If needed, cut strips in half, and layer additional sets.** Cut stacks of Star and Center Triangles until you have the total number needed. You may not need to cut the entire strip for the total number. Make a few extras, so imperfect pieces can be eliminated if necessary.

Overall Pattern			
	Cut	Into	Triangle Stacks
Wallhanging . . . 1	set	. . . . . .	10
Baby 1½	sets	. . . . .	26
Lap 2	sets	. . . . .	36
Twin 2½	sets	. . . . .	46
Double 3½	sets	. . . . .	64
Queen/King . . . 4½	sets	. . . . .	82

Pattern with Edge Blocks			
	Cut	Into	Triangle Stacks
Wallhanging . . . ¼	set	. . . .	2
Baby 1	set	. . . . . .	10
Lap 1	set	. . . . .	16
Twin 1½	sets	. . . . .	22
Double 2	sets	. . . . .	36
Queen/King . . . 2½	sets	. . . . .	50

12. Stack the triangles on the Square Up ruler as you layer cut, and place to the left of your sewing machine.

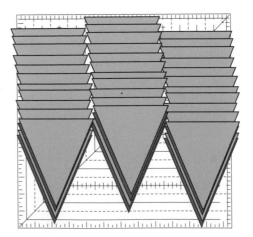

Four triangles are in each stack.
Center Triangles are on top.

Sewing Star and Center Triangles into Pairs

1. Apply the adhesive strip ¼" from your sewing machine needle.

2. Use your stiletto to separate the pairs, and pick up the first pair of triangles already right sides together.

   Carefully match outside edges!

3. Sew from the wide base end of the triangle, toward the point. Use your stiletto to guide the triangles.

   Maintain an accurate ¼" seam allowance.

4. Assembly-line sew the second pair after the first. It may be necessary to raise the presser foot and slip it in place to avoid jamming the machine. Assembly-line sew all paired triangles.

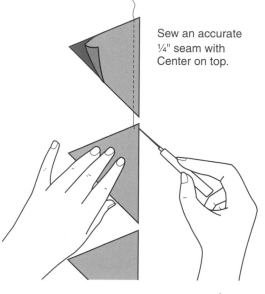

Sew an accurate ¼" seam with Center on top.

5. Snip the connecting threads and **stack with Star on top**.

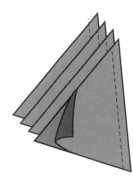

6. Open and fingerpress the seams toward the Star, or crease with a wooden iron. Stack into two piles.

   Do not press the Star/Center pairs with an iron at this time. Pressing distorts the bias cut on the sides of the triangles.

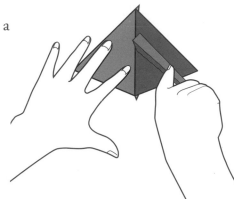

Sewing the Star/Center Pairs into Half Circles

1. Arrange two piles next to your sewing machine.

   Multi-Fabric Blocks: Mix the fabrics in your pairs.

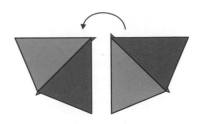

Notice direction of seam allowances.

Place this many in each pile:		
	Overall Pattern	Edge Block Pattern
Wallhanging	. . .10	2
Baby	26	10
Lap	36	16
Twin	46	22
Double	64	36
Queen/King	. . .82	50

2. Flip the right pair to the left pair, right sides together. Grasp the tips and roll match.

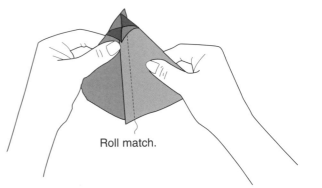

Roll match.

3. Wiggle-match the seams to interlock them. Fingerpress the **top seam up** toward the Star and the **underneath seam down** toward the Star.

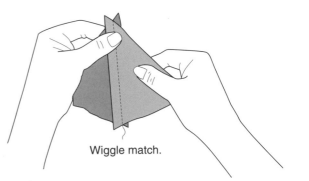

Wiggle match.

4. Stitch past the tip. Use the stiletto to get seams under presser foot. Stop. Match and fingerpin the base. Stitch to the end.

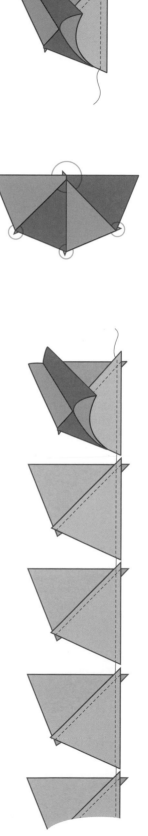

5. Open and check for the ¼" seam allowance and even outside edges (see circles). The top edge should be straight.

6. Assembly-line sew the next set of pairs, repeating the process until all pairs are sewn into half circles.

7. Clip the connecting threads.

    Do not press at this time. Pressing distorts the bias edges.

Sewing the Halves into Circles

1. Arrange two equal piles in this order next to your sewing machine.

   Multi-Fabric Blocks: Mix the fabrics in your half circles.

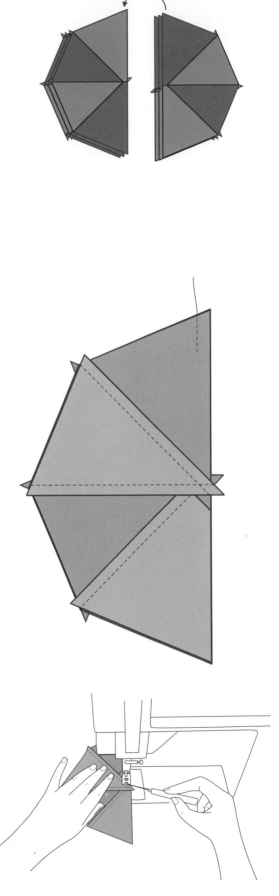

Place this many in each pile:		
	Overall Pattern	Edge Block Pattern
Wallhanging . . . 5		 1
Baby 13		5
Lap 18		8
Twin 23		11
Double 32		18
Queen/King . . .41		25

2. Flip the right piece to the left piece and anchor the outside edge with 1" of stitching.

3. Open center seam and wiggle-match to interlock. Fingerpress **seams toward Star, pushing seams flat on top and underneath.**

   Look for the indentations on the half underneath. Slip the points on the top half into those indentations.

4. Match and hold the seams flat at the center with your stiletto as you stitch. Sew from the outside edge across the center to the other outside edge.

5. The new stitching line must cross the intersection exactly to have a crisp center on the right side.

   Check on the back side to see if the stitching crossed the intersection also.

   The seam is bulky in the center. If necessary, restitch the center with a ¼" seam allowance.

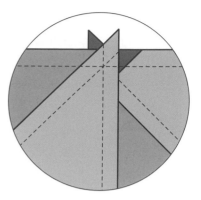

6. Open and look at the match from the right side.

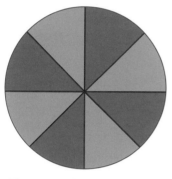

The center of the block should look like this.

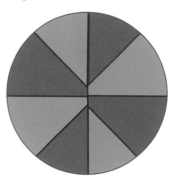

If the center looks like this, **decrease** the seam allowance.

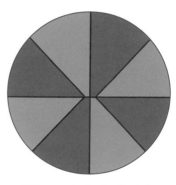

If the center looks like this, **increase** the seam allowance.

If you are not pleased with the match, you may choose to pin. See next page for pinning instructions.

7. Assembly-line sew all halves into circles.
8. Clip the connecting threads.

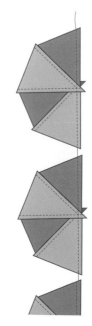

Pinning the Centers

If you are not satisfied with the match, you may choose to pin the center.

1. Remove one inch of stitches on either side of the center.

2. Push a pin through the top piece where the stitching crosses.

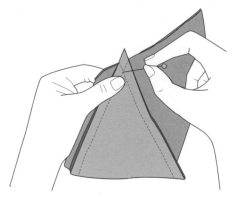

3. Push back seam to left. Flip the top half circle forward to expose the seam of the other pair.

4. Push the pin through at the intersection of the seams.

5. Stand the pin straight pushing the layers together. This standing pin holds the match in place.

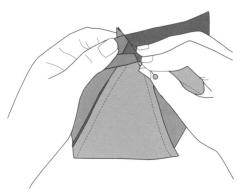

6. Hold the layers tightly at the standing pin and use a second pin to hold the match next to the standing pin.

7. Remove the standing pin.

8. Restitch.

9. Assembly-line sew all halves into circles.

10. Clip the connecting threads.

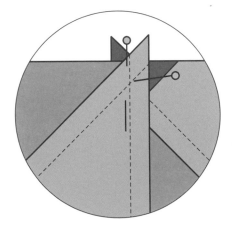

Making the Circle Lie Flat

1. With a stiletto or seam ripper, remove the four to five stitches perpendicular to the center seam.

2. Flip the block to the back, and remove the second set of four to five stitches.

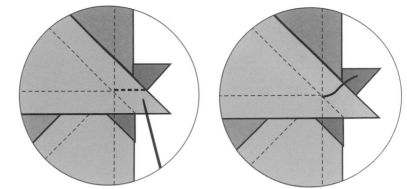

3. From the wrong side, fingerpress the center open and flat. The pressed seams create a "pinwheel" center, minimizing bulk.

4. Gently press the seams flat toward Star with iron.

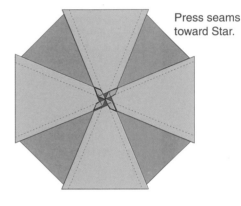

Press seams toward Star.

Checking the Outside Edges

1. Check to see if any outside edges are uneven.

2. **Sliver trim** any uneven outside edges by placing the Square Up ruler on top of the block, lining up the diagonal line across the center of the block and the edges of the ruler on the edges of the block. The seams should line up near 2½" and 6".

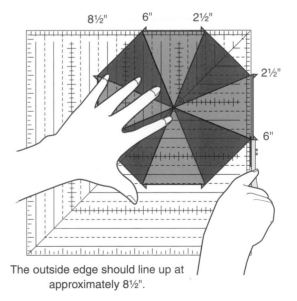

The outside edge should line up at approximately 8½".

Circles for the Star/Center blocks:

	Overall Pattern	Edge Block Pattern
Wallhanging	5	1
Baby	13	5
Lap	18	8
Twin	23	11
Double	32	18
Queen/King	41	25

Adding the Background Corner Triangles

1. Make two stacks of Background Corner Triangles, right side up, equal to the number of circle blocks.

    Multi-Fabric Blocks: Mix the fabrics in your triangles.

    Place next to the Star Triangles.

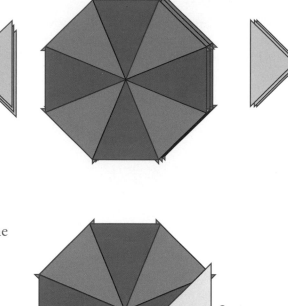

2. Flip and center a Corner Triangle right sides together to the base of the adjacent Star Triangle.

    The Corner Triangles are oversized, and are trimmed later.

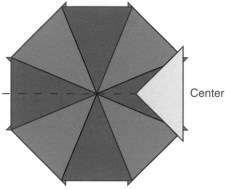

Center

3. Sew across the base. Overlap the second circle to assembly-line sew the second corner. Repeat with all circles.

4. Turn the string of circles around, and add the other corner to the opposite side.

5. Clip the connecting threads and stack.

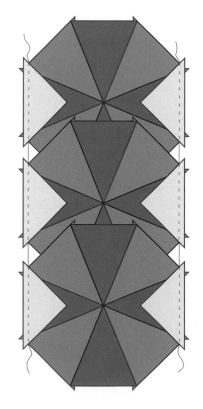

6. Arrange a second set of Background Corner triangles next to the Star triangles.

7. Assembly-line sew the remaining corners.

8. Clip apart.

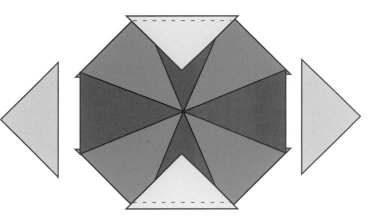

9. Press to set the seams. Open and press seams toward Corner Triangles.

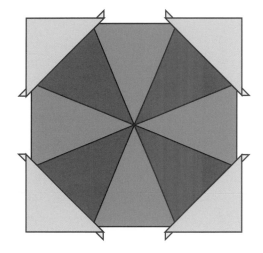

Squaring the Block

The blocks should be approximately **8½" square**.

The corners of the block are oversized and need to be trimmed.

It is important not to trim away any ¼" seam allowance on the corner seams.

1. Place the Square Up Ruler on top of the block. Line top and right edges of the ruler with two sides of the block.

   The lines ¼" from the edge of the ruler must line up with the seam allowances of the corners.

   Trim the corners.

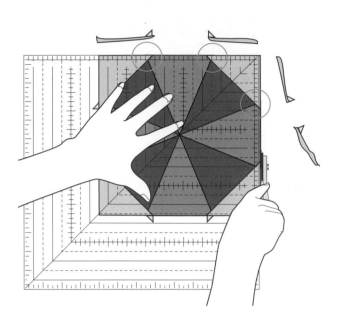

2. Lift the ruler, turn the block half way around, and trim the remaining corners of the block.

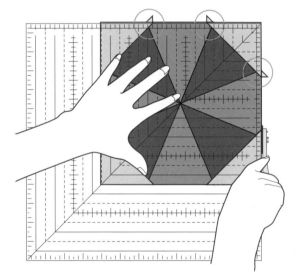

3. Trim all corners without removing the ¼" seam allowance. **It is more important to have the ¼" seam allowance than all of the blocks be exactly the same. It is easy to stretch or ease in an extra ⅛". The trimmed corners should be the same size.**

4. Square the remaining blocks.

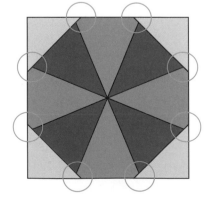

The Star/Background Blocks ②
Layer Cutting for Star/Background and Edge Blocks

1. Working from the bottom upward, layer **four 5" strips right sides together** on the pressing mat in this order:

   *Place a **Star strip** on the **bottom right side up**. Place a **Background strip** right sides together to the Star. Place a **second Star strip** on the **stack right side up**, and a **Background strip right sides together** to it. Four selvage to selvage strips are referred to as a Strip Set.*

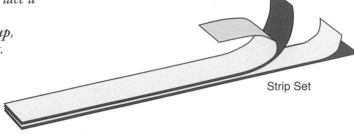
Strip Set

Multi-Fabric Blocks

Use variety in your fabrics when stacking strips.

2. Carefully line up the edges and left end selvages. Press.

3. Cut stacks with four triangles in each stack.

4. Layer additional sets of strips, and cut triangles from each strip set. You may not need to cut up the whole set of strips.

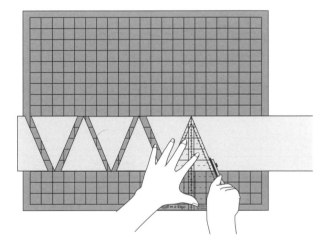

Overall Pattern			
	Cut	**Into**	**Triangle Stacks**
Wallhanging . . .	1 set		8
Baby	1½ sets		24
Lap	2 sets		34
Twin	3 sets		44
Double	3½ sets		62
Queen/King . . .	4½ sets		80

Pattern with Edge Blocks			
	Cut	**Into**	**Triangle Stacks**
Wallhanging . . .	1 set		12
Baby	1½ sets		30
Lap	2½ sets		41
Twin	3 sets		52
Double	3½ sets		71
Queen/King . . .	5 sets		92

Instructions For Edge Block Pattern Only

Look for the Edge Block Pattern on the side of the page to indicate instructions for the Edge Block Quilt. *(If you're making the Overall Quilt, or a variation without edge blocks, skip these instructions.)*

Saving Star Point for Edge Blocks with Star

1. Count out this many stacks of layered triangles:

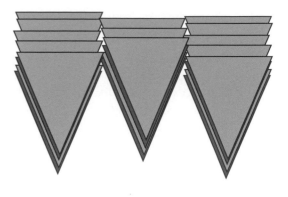

Wallhanging	. .2 stacks
Baby	. . . . . .4 stacks
Lap	. . . . . .5 stacks
Twin	. . . . . .6 stacks
Double	. . . . .7 stacks
Queen/King	. .8 stacks

2. Pin together with a slip of paper marked **page 53, Edge Blocks with Star**. Set aside.

Sewing Star and Background Triangles into Pairs

Overall Pattern and Remaining Triangles for Edge Blocks

1. Place the stacked triangles next to your sewing machine with Background on top.

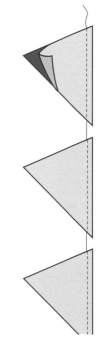

Stack this many:		
	Overall Pattern	Edge Block Pattern
Wallhanging	. . .8	10
Baby	24	26
Lap	34	36
Twin	44	46
Double	62	64
Queen/King	. . .80	84

2. Pick up the first pair of triangles already right sides together. Carefully match the edges.

3. Assembly-line sew all paired triangles from the wide base end toward the point.

4. Snip the connecting threads.

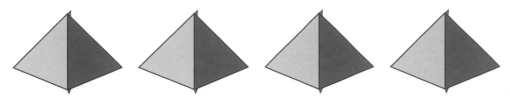

1. Count out four pairs.

2. Pin together with a slip of paper marked **page 56, Corner Blocks**.

3. Set aside.

Sewing the Star/Background Pairs into Half Circles

Overall Pattern and Remaining Triangles for Edge Blocks

1. Open and stack the pairs into two equal piles, fingerpressing seams toward the Star.

Stack this many in each pile:		
	Overall Pattern	Edge Block Pattern
Wallhanging	. . .8	8
Baby	24	24
Lap	34	34
Twin	44	44
Double	62	62
Queen/King	. . .80	82

2. Flip the right pair to the left pair. Check for fabric variety.

3. Fingerpress the top seam up, toward the Star, and underneath seam down, toward the Star.

4. Assembly-line sew all pairs into half circles.

Wallhanging - skip to page 47.

Sewing the Halves into Circles

1. Arrange two equal piles in this order next to your sewing machine.

   Multi-Fabric Blocks

   Mix the fabrics in your half circles.

Place this many in each pile:		
	Overall Pattern	Edge Block Pattern
Wallhanging	4	0
Baby	12	4
Lap	17	7
Twin	22	10
Double	31	17
Queen/King	40	24

Edge Blocks

Carefully count out half circles as instructed. Do not sew all half circles into whole circles.

2. Flip the right piece to the left piece, matching center seams.

3. Fingerpress seams toward Star, pushing seams flat on top and underneath.

4. Assembly-line sew.

5. Create "pinwheel" center, and press flat. Check outside edges and sliver trim if necessary.

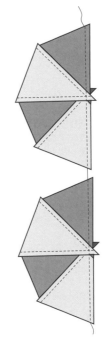

Circles for Star/Background Blocks		
	Overall Pattern	Edge Block Pattern
Wallhanging	4	0
Baby	12	4
Lap	17	7
Twin	22	10
Double	31	17
Queen/King	40	24

If you made extras, use the best blocks in your quilt.

Adding the Background Corner Triangles

1. Count out four piles of Background Corner Triangles, each equal to the number of circles.

2. Sew the Background Corner Triangles to the Background Center Triangles in this order:

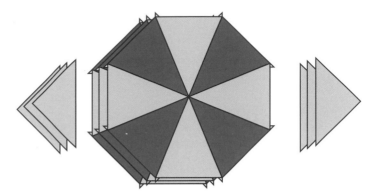

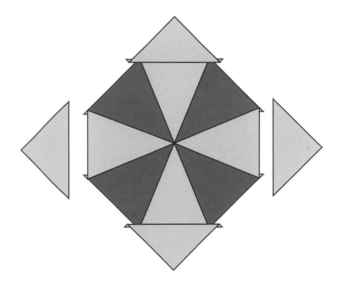

Squaring the Block

The blocks should be approximately **8½" square**.

The corners of the block are oversized and need to be trimmed.

It is important not to trim away any ¼" seam allowance on the seams.

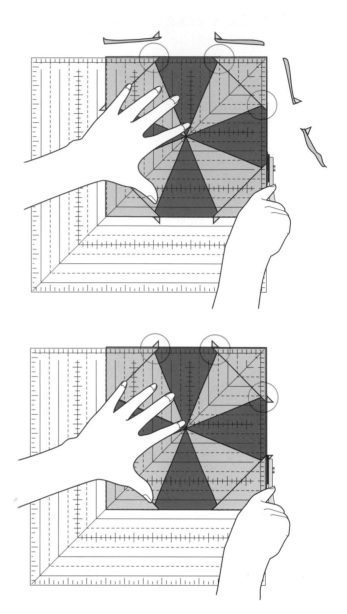

1. Place the Square Up Ruler on top of the block. Line two edges of the ruler with two sides of the block.

   The lines ¼" from the edge of the ruler must line up with the seam allowances of the corners. Trim the corners.

2. Lift the ruler, turn the block half way around, and trim the remaining corners of the block.

3. Trim all corners and sides without removing the ¼" seam allowance. **It is more important to have the ¼" seam allowance than all of the blocks be exactly the same. It is easy to stretch or ease in an extra ⅛".** **The trimmed corners should be the same size.**

4. Square the remaining blocks.

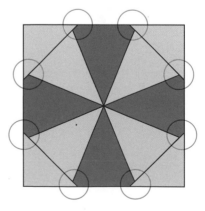

Overall Pattern

Star/Center and Star/Background Blocks are now done for the Overall Pattern. Skip over to page 58 for Sewing the Top Together.

The Edge Blocks

The Center of the quilt is made from the Star/Center Block and the Star/Background Block.

 ① Star / Center Block   ② Star / Background Block

Three additional blocks with different colorations are now made to complete the Edge Block pattern.

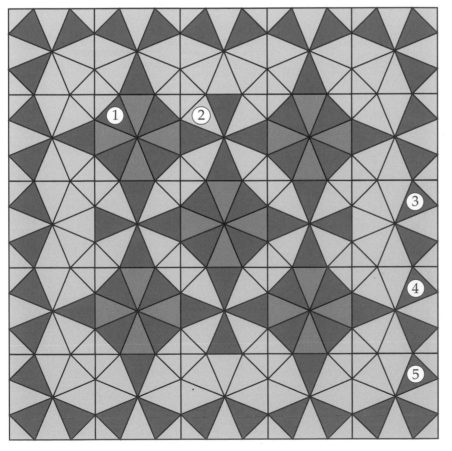

 ③ Edge Block without Star

 ④ Edge Block with Star

 ⑤ Corner Block

Layer Cutting Background Triangles for Edge Blocks

1. Working from the bottom upward, **layer four 5" Background strips right sides together** on the pressing mat in this order:

   *Place a **Background strip** on the **bottom right side up**. Place another **Background strip** right sides together to the first Background strip. Repeat with two more Background strips right sides together. Line up the left end selvages. Press.*

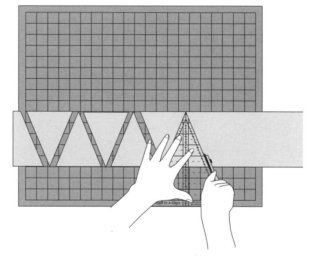

Wallhanging: Layer four half strips.

2. Repeat the cutting process as in the other triangles. Each stack has four triangles, or two pairs each already right sides together and ready for sewing.

3. Queen/King needs an additional layered half strip set.

Cut this many triangle stacks:	
Wallhanging	4
Baby	10
Lap	13
Twin	16
Double	19
Queen/King	24

Sewing Background and Background Triangles into Pairs

1. Place the stacked triangles next to your sewing machine.

2. Pick up the first pair of triangles already right sides together. Carefully match the edges.

3. Assembly-line sew all paired triangles from the wide base end toward the point.

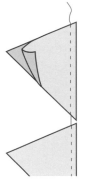

4. Snip the connecting threads.

5. Open and fingerpress or crease seam with a wooden iron.

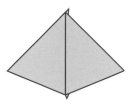

6. Use as needed for remaining blocks:

   ③ Edge Blocks without Star - page 50.

   ④ Edge Blocks with Star - page 53.

   ⑤ Corner Blocks - page 56.

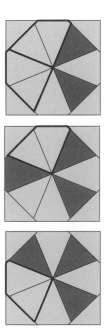

Wallhanging, skip to page 53.

Making Edge Blocks without Star ③
Sewing the Background/Background Pairs into Half Circles

1. Make two stacks using Background/Background pairs.

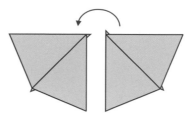

Place this many in each stack:
Wallhanging 0
Baby 4
Lap 6
Twin 8
Double 10
Queen/King 14

2. Flip the right piece to the left piece, matching outside edges and center seams.

3. Fingerpress the top seams flat and up, and the underneath seams flat and down.

4. Assembly-line sew.

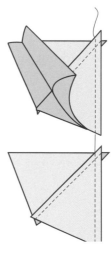

Sewing Two Halves Together

1. Count out an equal number of Background/Star half circles.

2. Arrange the two stacks next to your sewing machine in this order:

3. Flip the right piece to the left piece, matching outside edges and roll-matching center seams.

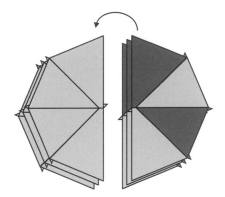

4. Fingerpress the **top seams flat toward the Star**, and the **underneath seams flat toward the Background**.

5. Assembly-line sew.

6. Create a "pinwheel" center, and press flat.

7. Check the outside edges and sliver trim if necessary.

   You need this many circles for Edge Blocks without Star:

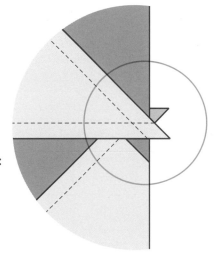

Edge Blocks without Stars	
Wallhanging 0	
Baby 4	
Lap 6	
Twin 8	
Double 10	
Queen/King 14	

Adding the Background Corner Triangles

1. Count out four piles of Background Corner Triangles, each equal to the number of circles.

2. Sew Background Corner Triangles to Star and Background Triangles in this order:

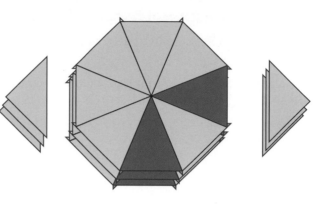

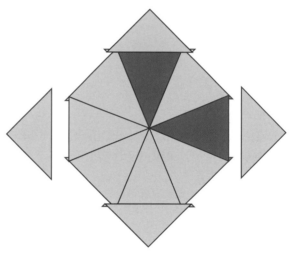

3. Press and square the Edge Blocks without Stars.

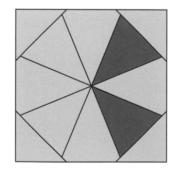

Making Edge Blocks with Star ④
Making the Star Half Circle

1. Use the reserved Star/Background pairs set aside on page 42.

2. Turn the stacks over so **Star is on the top**. Place the stacked triangles next to your sewing machine.

3. Pick up the first pair of triangles already right sides together. Carefully match the edges. Sew from the wide base end of the triangle, toward the point.

4. Assembly-line sew all paired triangles.

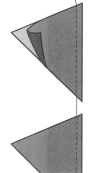

5. Open and fingerpress seam toward Background triangle.

Pairs for Edge Blocks	
Wallhanging	4 pairs
Baby	8 pairs
Lap	10 pairs
Twin	12 pairs
Double	14 pairs
Queen/King	16 pairs

6. Make two stacks using Background/Background pairs and Star/Background pairs.

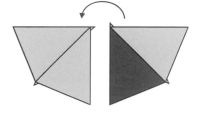

Place this many in each stack:	
Wallhanging	4
Baby	8
Lap	10
Twin	12
Double	14
Queen/King	16

7. Flip the right piece to the left piece, matching outside edges and center seams.

8. Fingerpress the top seams up and flat toward the Background, and the underneath seams down and flat.

9. Assembly-line sew.

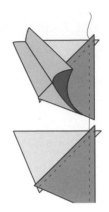

Sewing Two Halves Together

1. Count out an equal number of Background/Star half circles.

2. Arrange the two stacks next to your sewing machine in this order:

3. Flip the right piece to the left piece, matching outside edges and roll-matching center seams.

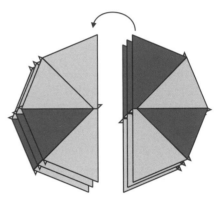

4. Fingerpress the top seams flat toward the Star, and the underneath seams toward the Background and flat.

5. Assembly-line sew.

6. Create "pinwheel" centers, and press. One seam of Star can not be pressed toward the Star.

7. Check outside edges and sliver trim if necessary.

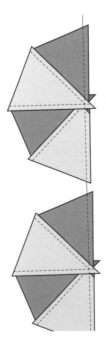

Adding the Background Corner Triangles

1. Count out four piles of
   Background Corner Triangles, each
   equal to the number of circles.

2. Sew Background Corner Triangles
   to Center Triangles in this order:

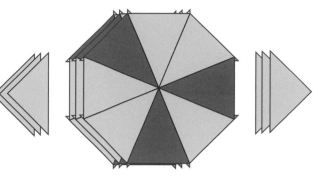

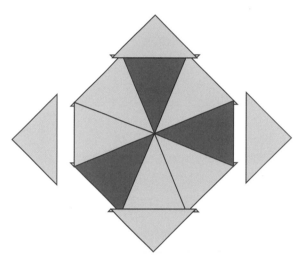

3. Press and square
   the Edge Blocks with Star.

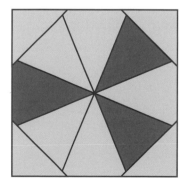

Making Four Corner Blocks ⑤

Making the Corner Halves

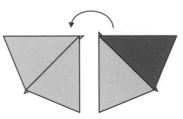

1. Make two stacks with four pairs in each, using reserved Background/Background pairs with Background/Star pairs.

2. Arrange in this order:

3. Flip the right piece to the left piece, matching outside edges and center seams.

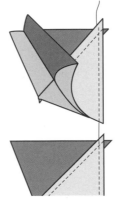

4. Fingerpress the top seams up and flat, and the underneath seams down and flat.

5. Assembly-line sew.

Sewing Two Halves Together

1. Count out four Background/Star half circles.

2. Arrange the two stacks next to your sewing machine in this order:

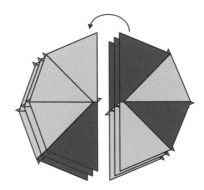

3. Flip the right piece to the left piece, matching outside edges and roll-matching center seams.

4. Fingerpress the top seams flat toward the Star, and the underneath seams flat toward the Background.

5. Assembly-line sew.

6. Create a "pinwheel" center, and press flat.

7. Check outside edges and sliver trim if necessary.

Adding the Background Corner Triangles

1. Count out four piles of Corner Triangles, each with four in them.

2. Sew Background Corner Triangles to Center Triangles in this order:

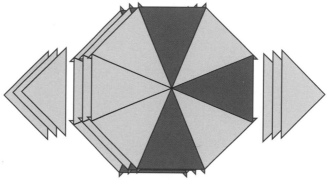

3. Press and square the Corner Blocks.

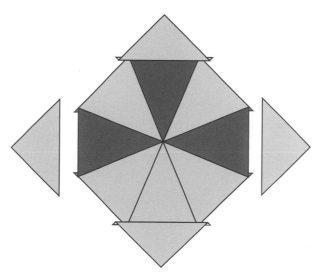

Sewing the Top Together

Stacking the Vertical Rows

1. Lay out the blocks following the diagram for your size quilt, pages 62-67.

Blocks	Across	Down
Wallhanging	3	3
Baby	5	5
Lap	5	7
Twin	5	9
Double	7	9
Queen/King	9	9

Example of Overall Baby Quilt

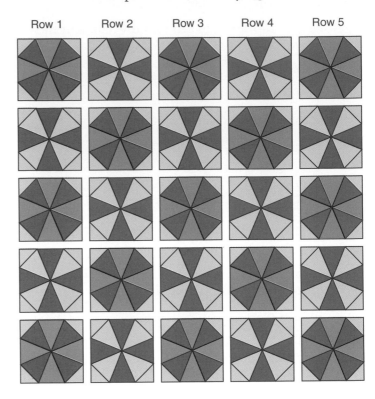

Row 1   Row 2   Row 3   Row 4   Row 5

2. Flip the second vertical row right sides together onto the first vertical row.

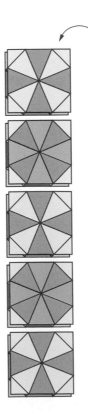

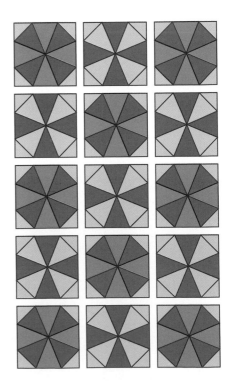

3. Pick up and stack the pairs of blocks starting at the top. The pair at the top will be on top of the stack.

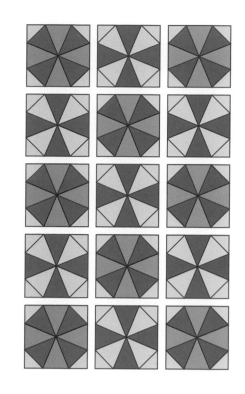

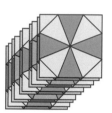

4. Stack each of the vertical rows from the top to the bottom, having the top block on the top of the stack each time.

5. Write the row number on a piece of paper and pin it through all thicknesses of fabric.

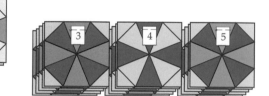

Sewing the Vertical Seams

Start with the stack of paired blocks from Row 1 and 2. Lay the stack next to your sewing machine.

1. Pick up top paired blocks.

2. Match and pin the seams together. Stretch or ease the triangles to fit.

3. Match the outside edges, backstitch, and stitch across the seams. Use the stiletto to hold the seams flat as you stitch across them.

4. Match the outside edges.

5. Do not cut the threads or lift the presser foot.

6. Pick up the next pair of blocks. Butt them right behind the first two.

7. Anchor the two with ½" of stitching. Fingerpin or pin the seams and corners of the blocks. Stretch or ease the blocks to fit.

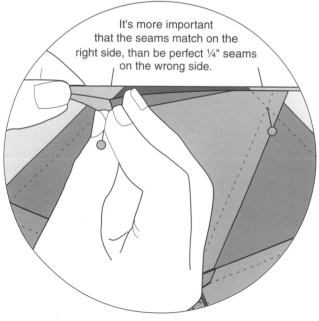

It's more important that the seams match on the right side, than be perfect ¼" seams on the wrong side.

8. Continue butting and sewing blocks together until Row 1 and 2 are completed.

9. Do not cut the blocks apart.

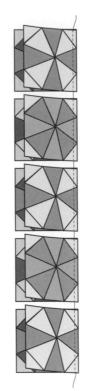

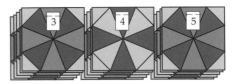

Adding the Third Vertical Row

1. Place the stacked third vertical row of blocks to the right of your sewing machine.

2. Open the chained pair of blocks. Make sure they are in the right arrangement.

3. Flip the block on the top of the third row right sides together to the top block on the second row.

4. Backstitch, pin or fingerpin the match points, and sew.

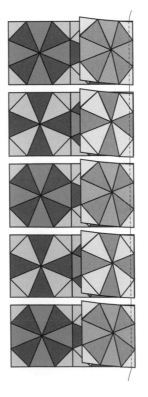

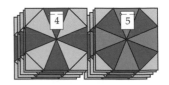

60

5. Continue sewing all blocks in all vertical rows in the same manner.

   Do not clip the threads holding the blocks together.

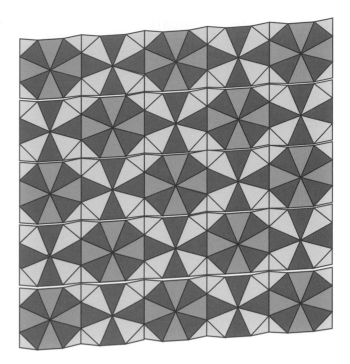

Sewing the Horizontal Rows

1. Flip the top row down onto the second row with right sides together. Match, pin, ease, and stitch together. Where the two blocks are joined by a thread, match the seam carefully. Push the vertical seam allowances in opposite directions.

2. Stitch all horizontal rows in the same manner, keeping the vertical seam allowances pushed in the same direction.

3. Press the quilt top from the wrong side first and then the right side.

4. Check that corners are square and edges are straight. Trim if necessary.

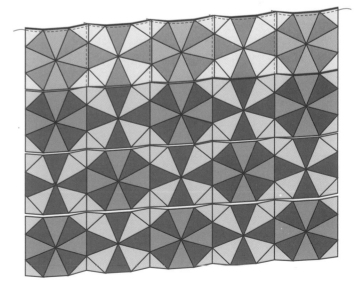

Wallhanging Overall

 ① Star/Center
Make 5

 ② Star/Background
Make 4

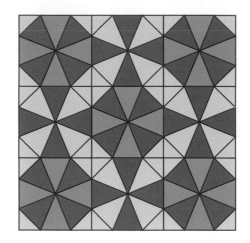

Wallhanging Edge Blocks

 ① Star/Center
Make 1

 ④ Edge Blocks with Star
Make 4

 ⑤ Corner Blocks
Make 4

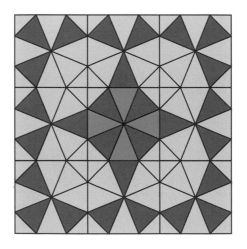

Baby Overall

 ① Star/Center
Make 13

 ② Star/Background
Make 12

Baby Edge Blocks

 ① Star/Center
Make 5

 ② Star/Background
Make 4

 ③ Edge Blocks without Star
Make 4

 ④ Edge Blocks with Star
Make 8

 ⑤ Corner Blocks
Make 4

Lap Overall

 ① Star/Center
Make 18

 ② Star/Background
Make 17

Lap Edge Blocks

 ① Star/Center
Make 8

 ② Star/Background
Make 7

 ③ Edge Blocks without Star
Make 6

 ④ Edge Blocks with Star
Make 10

 ⑤ Corner Blocks
Make 4

Twin Overall

 ① Star/Center
Make 23

 ② Star/Background
Make 22

Twin Edge Blocks

 ① Star/Center
Make 11

 ② Star/Background
Make 10

 ③ Edge Blocks without Star
Make 8

 ④ Edge Blocks with Star
Make 12

⑤ Corner Blocks
Make 4

Double Overall

 ① Star/Center
Make 32

 ② Star/Background
Make 31

Double Edge Blocks

 ① Star/Center
Make 18

 ② Star/Background
Make 17

 ③ Edge Blocks without Star
Make 10

 ④ Edge Blocks with Star
Make 14

 ⑤ Corner Blocks
Make 4

Queen/King Overall

 ① Star/Center
Make 41

 ② Star/Background
Make 40

Queen/King Edge Blocks

 ① Star/Center
Make 25

 ② Star/Background
Make 24

 ③ Edge Blocks without Star
Make 12

 ④ Edge Blocks with Star
Make 16

 ⑤ Corner Blocks
Make 4

Adding the Borders

Creativity in Border Sizes

Suggested border yardage and border examples are given for each quilt. However, you may wish to custom design the borders by changing the widths of the strips. This might change yardage for backing, binding, and batting.

When custom fitting the quilt, lay the top on your bed before adding the borders and backing. Measure to find how much border is needed to get the fit you want. Keep in mind that a large quilt will shrink approximately 3" in the length and width after machine quilting.

Piecing the Strips for Border and Binding

1. Stack and square off the ends of each strip, trimming away the selvage edges.

2. Seam the strips of each fabric into one long piece by assembly-line sewing.

   Lay the first strip right side up. Lay the second strip right sides to it. Backstitch, stitch the short ends together, and backstitch again.

   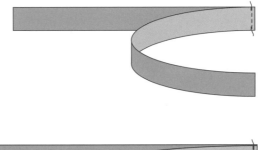

   Take the strip on the top and fold it so the right side is up. Place the third strip right sides to it, backstitch and stitch, and backstitch again.

3. Clip the threads holding the strips together.

   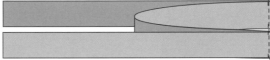

4. Press seams to one side.

First Border

1. Measure down the center of the quilt to find the length. Cut two strips that measurement plus two inches.

2. Right sides together, match and pin the center of the strips to the center of the sides. Extend one inch of strip on each end. Be sure to pin at the ends and intermittently along the sides.

3. Sew ¼" seam allowance **with the quilt on top**.

4. Press to set the closed seam.

5. Open and press, directing the seams toward the border.

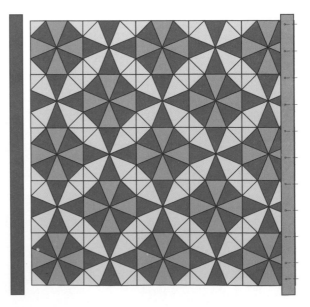

6. Square the ends even with the top and bottom edges of the quilt.

7. Measure the width across the center including the newly added border. Cut two strips that measurement plus two inches.

8. Right sides together, match and pin the center of the strips to the center of the top and bottom edges of the quilt. Extend one inch of strip on each end. Pin at the ends and along the width of the border.

9. Sew with the quilt on top.

10. Press, directing the seams toward the border.

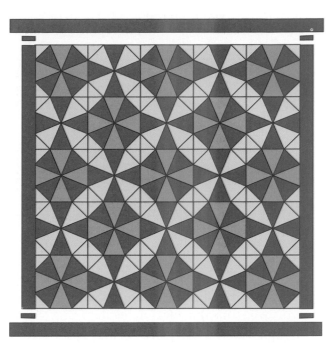

11. Square the ends even with the side borders.

12. Repeat with each border.

13. Press the quilt top.

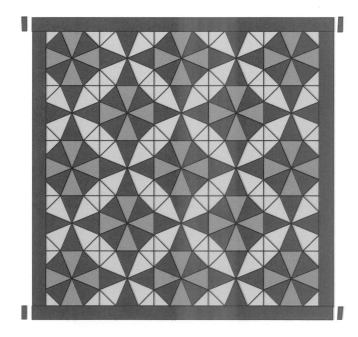

Folded Border

A Folded Border is a folded, narrow strip of fabric that can be sewn between any two borders for accent color.

1. Plan the placement of the Folded Border.

2. Cut enough 1½" strips to fit around the quilt.

3. Assembly-line sew the narrow strips together.

4. Press the strip in half lengthwise, wrong sides together.

5. Measure the sides of the quilt, and cut two strips this measurement.

6. Match and pin raw edges of quilt and Folded Border. Sew with a seam two threads less than ¼". Use a long stitch or 10 stitches per inch.

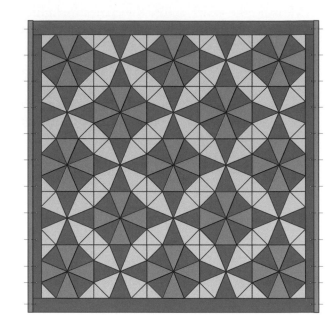

7. Measure top and bottom, and cut two strips this measurement.

8. Pin and sew to the quilt. Do not fold out.

9. Add additional borders.

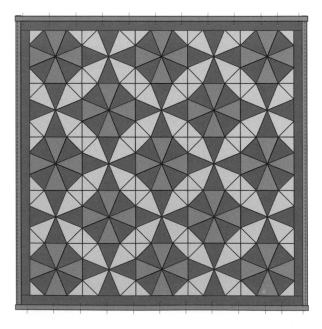

Machine Quilting
Layering Quilt Top with Backing and Batting

1. Piece the backing yardage together for larger size quilts.

   The seams may run down the center back or across the width, whichever works better for your yardage. If the backing is smaller than the quilt top, piece extra fabric together and sew into the center seam to make it large enough. A row of extra blocks down the center back also adds interest. The backing can then look as creative as the front.

2. Stretch out the backing right side down on a large floor area or table. Tape down on a floor area or clamp onto a table with large binder clips.

3. Place and smooth out the batting on top.

4. Place the quilt top right side up and centered on top of the batting. Completely smooth and stretch all layers until they are flat.

5. Re-tape or clip securely. The backing and batting should extend at least 2" on all sides.

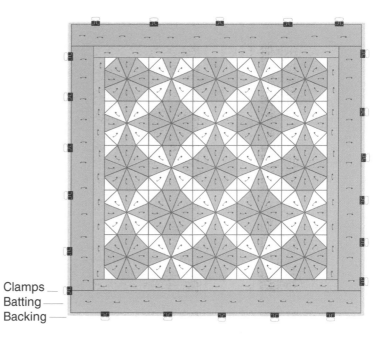

Clamps —
Batting —
Backing —

Quick and Easy Safety Pinning

1. Place 1" safety pins throughout the quilt away from the seams, in each Star and Center triangle.

2. Begin pinning in the center and work to the outside.

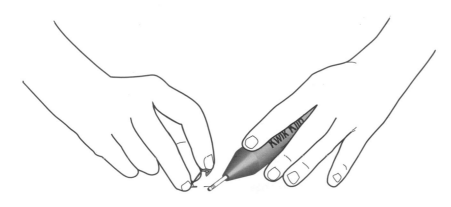

Grasp the opened pin in your right hand and the pinning tool in your left hand. Push the pin through the three layers, and bring the tip of the pin back out. Catch the tip in the groove of the tool and allow point to extend far enough to push pin closure down.

Machine Quilting around the Background Triangles

1. Place a walking foot attachment on your machine for "Stitch in the Ditch" quilting.

2. Place invisible thread in the top of your machine, or regular thread to match your Background. Loosen the top tension if using invisible thread.

3. Place regular thread in the bobbin to match the backing.

4. Lengthen your stitch to 8-10 stitches per inch, or a #3 or #4 setting.

   The easiest seams to follow when machine quilting are the seams from the Background triangles.

   Sew a long curved, continuous line on one side of the Background from one side of the quilt to the other.

   Repeat on the opposite side of the Background seam.

   Optional: Machine quilt or bar tack the center of each star.

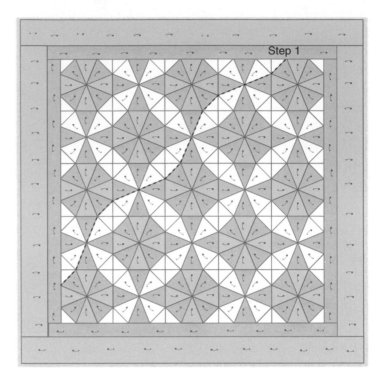

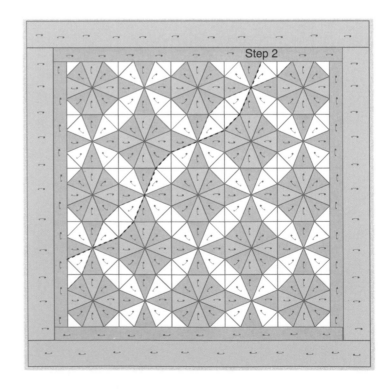

5. Roll the quilt diagonally from the outside edge in toward middle. Hold this roll with quilt clips or pins.

6. Slide this roll into the keyhole of the sewing machine.

7. Place the needle in the depth of the seam and pull up the bobbin thread. Lock your thread with ½" of tiny stitches when you begin and end your sewing line. Trim the threads after you lock the stitches.

8. Run your hand underneath to feel for puckers.

9. Place your hands flat on both sides of the needle. Keep the quilt area flat and tight. If you need to ease in the top fabric, feed the quilt through the machine by pushing the layers of fabric and batting forward underneath the walking foot.

10. Unroll, roll, and machine quilt on all diagonal lines.

11. "Stitch in the Ditch" through all border seams.

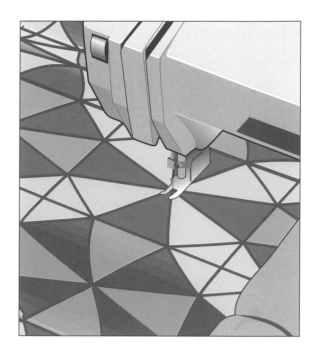

Edge Block Pattern

Follow the lines of the outside blocks.

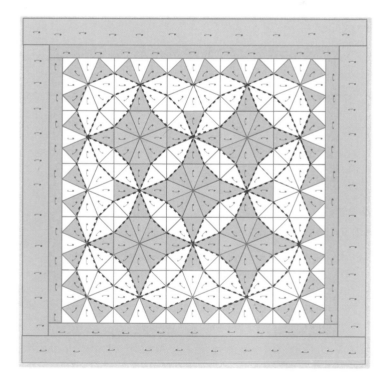

If puckering occurs, remove the stitching by grasping the bobbin thread with a pin or tweezers and pull gently to expose the invisible thread. Touch the invisible thread stitches with the rotary cutter blade as you pull the bobbin thread free from the quilt. Re-sew.

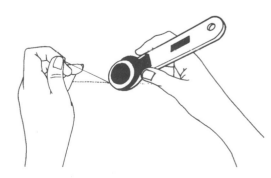

Free Motion Stippling

Free motion stippling is overall meandering stitches that "fill" the Background, or Star Center, or Star Points.

Machine Set Up

1. Refer to your instruction manual for directions on how to darn with your machine. Use a darning foot or spring needle, and drop the feed dogs or cover with a plate.

2. No stitch length is required as you control the length. Use a fine needle and a little hole throat plate with a center needle position. Use invisible or regular thread in the top and regular thread to match the backing in the bobbin. Loosen the top tension if using invisible thread.

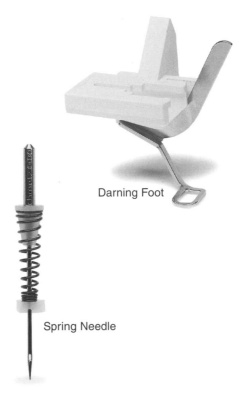

Darning Foot

Spring Needle

Practice

Set up a practice swatch of the three layers to become comfortable with moving the fabric to make your desired size stitch. Adjust the tension for either invisible or regular thread. Practice moving your hands back and forward and sideways, but not turning the swatch. The only requirements for stippling are not to sew across a stippled line of stitching or across the patchwork.

Stippling Your Quilt

1. Bring the bobbin thread up ¼" away from the Background. Lower the needle into the Background and drop the foot. Moving the fabric very slowly, take a few tiny stitches to lock them. Snip off the tails of the threads.

2. With your eyes watching the outline of the block ahead of the needle, and your fingertips stretching the fabric and acting as a quilting hoop, move the fabric in a steady motion while the machine is running at a constant speed. Keep the top of the quilt in the same position by moving the fabric underneath the needle side to side, and forward and backward.

3. Lock off the tiny stitches and clip the threads at the end of the block.

Adding the Binding

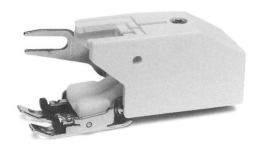

Use a walking foot attachment and regular thread on top and in the bobbin to match the binding. Use 10 stitches per inch, or #3 setting.
See page 68 to make one long binding strip.

1. Press the binding strip in half lengthwise with right sides out.

2. Line up the raw edges of the folded binding with the raw edge of the quilt top at the middle of one side.

3. Begin sewing 4" from the end of the binding.

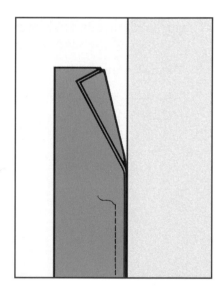

4. At the corner, stop the stitching ¼" from the edge with the needle in the fabric. Raise the presser foot and turn the quilt to the next side. Put the foot back down.

5. Sew backwards ¼" to the edge of the binding, raise the foot, and pull the quilt forward slightly.

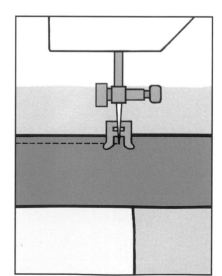

6. Fold the binding strip straight up on the diagonal. Fingerpress in the diagonal fold.

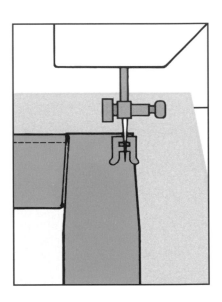

7. Fold the binding strip straight down with the diagonal fold underneath. Line up the top of the fold with the raw edge of the binding underneath.

8. Begin sewing from the corner.

9. Continue sewing and mitering the corners around the outside of the quilt.

10. Stop sewing 4" from where the ends will overlap.

11. Line up the two ends of binding. Trim the excess with a ½" overlap.

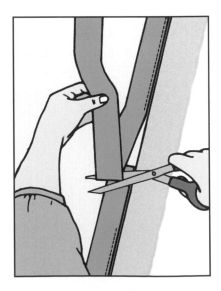

12. Open out the folded ends and pin right sides together. Sew a ¼" seam.

13. Continue to sew the binding in place.

14. Trim the batting and backing up to the raw edges of the binding.

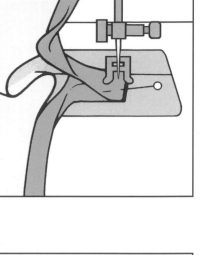

15. Fold the binding to the backside of the quilt. Pin in place so that the folded edge on the binding covers the stitching line. Tuck in the excess fabric at each miter on the diagonal.

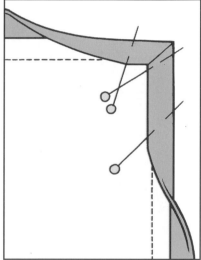

16. From the right side, "stitch in the ditch" using invisible thread on the right side, and a bobbin thread to match the binding on the back side. Catch the folded edge of the binding on the back side with the stitching.

    Optional: Slipstitch the binding in place by hand.

17. Sew an identification label on the backing.

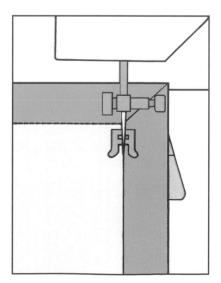

Creative Kaleidoscopes

Once you have mastered the construction of the Kaleidoscope Block, you may want to sew one of the creative color variations pictured on pages 85-88. Yardage charts and instructions for each quilt are included. Follow these general sewing instructions or design your own using chart provided on page 84.

General Instructions

1. Each block is divided by heavy lines into four pairs.

2. Each pair has a left and right side.

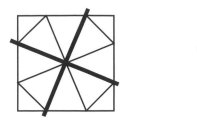

3. **Fabric strips are strategically layered** so when triangle cutting and sewing is completed, triangles are correctly placed on left or right side. The fabric strip for the pair's **left triangle must be on the bottom, right side up**. The fabric strip for the **right triangle is always placed on top**, right sides together to the bottom strip.

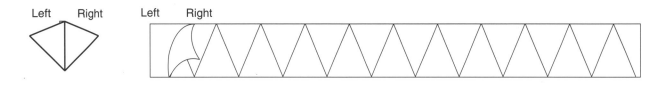

4. Count identical pairs from all blocks.

5. Cut layered pairs from fabric strips.

6. Sew pairs together, wide end to narrow.

7. Fingerpress seams to lay behind left triangle.

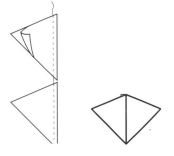

8. Lay out one block at a time, or stack multiples of the same block.

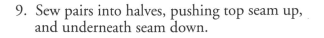

9. Sew pairs into halves, pushing top seam up, and underneath seam down.

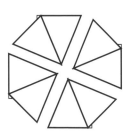
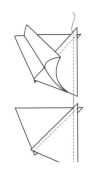

10. Sew halves into wholes, matching centers and pushing seams flat.

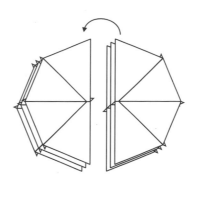

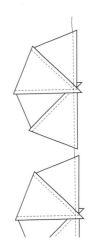

11. Make a "pinwheel" and press flat.
12. Following each block, sew on the corners.

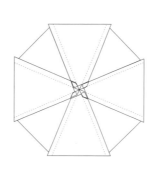

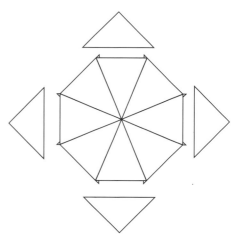

13. Square each block.
14. Sew top together and finish.

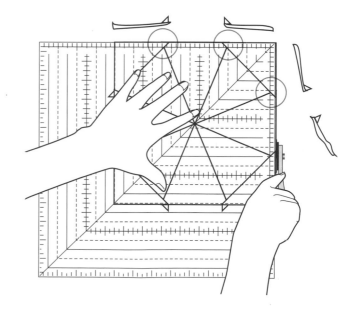

Regal Beauty, *see color photo page 85*

Three Fabrics

Cut strips selvage to selvage.

■ Fabric 1 - 1½ yds - Star
    (3) 5" strips
Second Border
    (5) 4" strips
Binding
    (4) 3" strips

■ Fabric 2 - ⅝ yd - Center
    (2) 5" strips
Folded Border
    (4) 1¼" strips

□ Fabric 3 - 1⅛ yds - Background
    (2) 5" strips
    (2) 4" strips
       (18) 4" squares, then cut on diagonal
First Border
    (4) 5" strips

Fusible Interfacing - ¼ yd.
    (1) 5" strip

Backing - 3 yds
    (2) equal pieces
Batting - 54" square

Layer strips right sides together.
Cut triangles and sew these pairs:

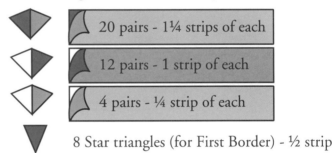

20 pairs - 1¼ strips of each

12 pairs - 1 strip of each

4 pairs - ¼ strip of each

8 Star triangles (for First Border) - ½ strip

Sew Pairs into Blocks

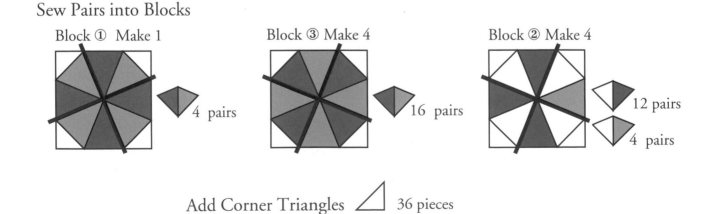

Block ① Make 1   4 pairs

Block ③ Make 4   16 pairs

Block ② Make 4   12 pairs   4 pairs

Add Corner Triangles   36 pieces

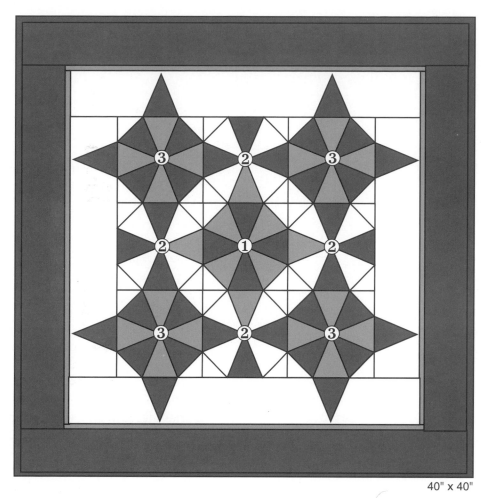

40" x 40"

Adding Eight Border Triangles

1. Cut eight Star triangles.

2. Place right sides of triangles against rough, fusible side of interfacing.

3. Sew ¼" seam around two equal sides.

4. Cut apart, trim and turn right side out. Use stiletto to pull out points.

5. Sew nine blocks together into top.

6. Pin interfaced triangles right sides together to quilt, matching open end of triangle to edge of fabric.

7. Pin and sew 5" strips of First Border on two opposite sides. Fuse triangles in place.

8. Stitch around two equal sides of triangle by hand or by machine with invisible thread and blind hem stitch.

9. Pin triangles and sew borders to top and bottom, enclosing base of triangles in seams. Fuse and sew triangles to border.

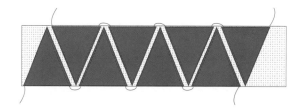

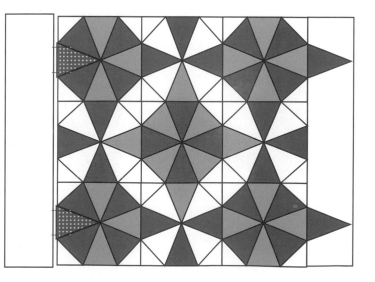

Stained Glass Prism, *see color photo page 85*

Three Fabrics

Cut strips selvage to selvage.

■ **Fabric 1 - 1¾ yds**
    (2) 5" strips
    (2) 4" strips
      (20) 4" squares, then cut on diagonal
   Second Border
    (5) 4" strips
   Binding
    (5) 3" strips

□ **Fabric 2 - 1¾ yds**
    (9) 5" strips
    (3) 4" strips
      (26) 4" squares, then cut on diagonal

■ **Fabric 3 - ¾ yd**
    (2) 5" strips
    (1) 4" strip
      (4) 4" squares, then cut on diagonal
   First Border
    (4) 2" strips

   Backing - 3 yds
    (2) equal pieces
   Batting - 54" square

Layer strips right sides together.
Cut triangles and sew these pairs:

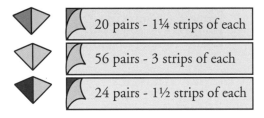

20 pairs - 1¼ strips of each
56 pairs - 3 strips of each
24 pairs - 1½ strips of each

Sew Pairs into Blocks

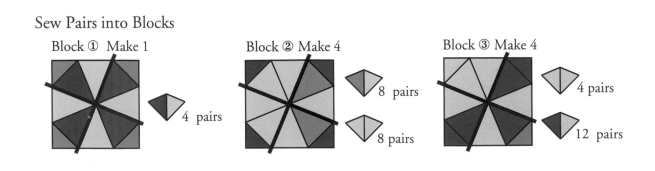

Block ① Make 1   4 pairs

Block ② Make 4   8 pairs   8 pairs

Block ③ Make 4   4 pairs   12 pairs

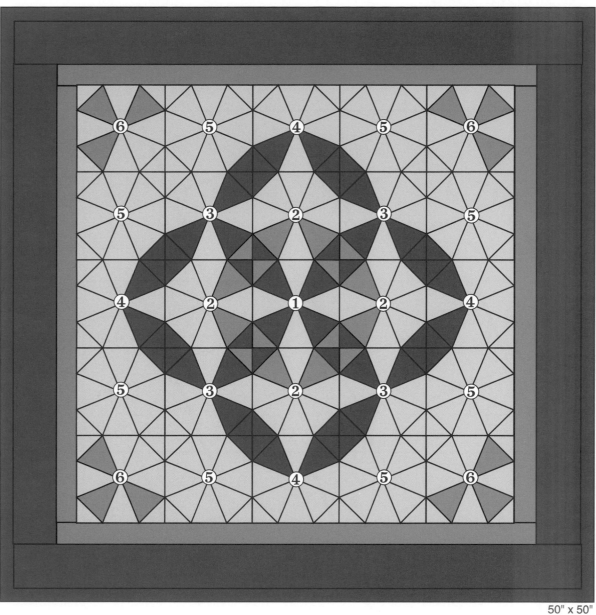

50" x 50"

Block ④ Make 4

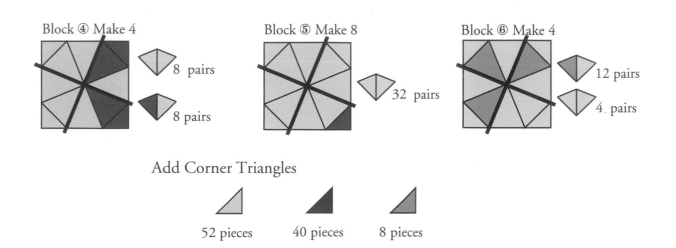

8 pairs

8 pairs

Block ⑤ Make 8

32 pairs

Block ⑥ Make 4

12 pairs

4 pairs

Add Corner Triangles

52 pieces   40 pieces   8 pieces

Color in your own nine block design.

Arrows indicates direction to flip triangle.

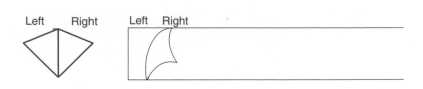

Left   Right

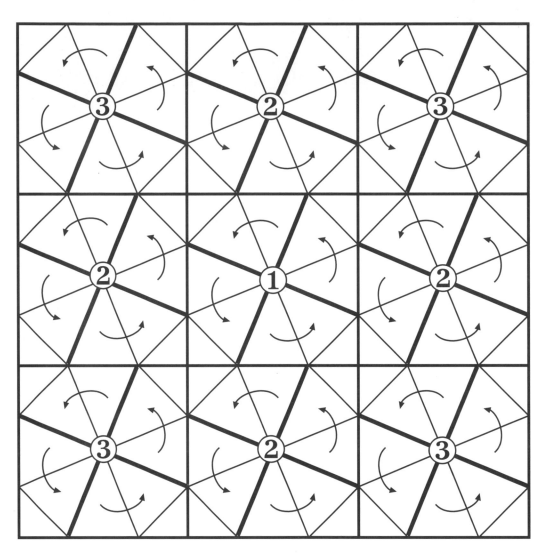

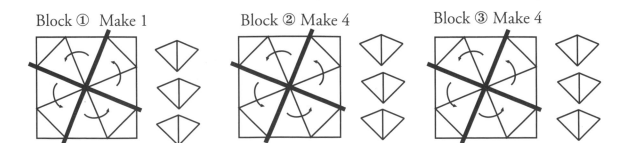

Block ① Make 1   Block ② Make 4   Block ③ Make 4

Regal Beauty
Nine Block Wallhanging
by Patricia Knoechel

A crisp white background bordered by a cool navy blue fabric clearly defines the stars in this dramatic wallhanging. A folded 1½" border of burgundy fabric adds a sophisticated touch. *See instructions on page 80.*

Prairie Sunburst
Nine Block Wallhanging
by Teresa Varnes

A sunburst of kaleidoscope colors appear in this nine block wallhanging. The fine-textured print and muted colors of purple, turquoise and moss green give this wallhanging a classic look. *See instructions on page 89.*

Stained Glass Prism
Twenty-five Block Quilt
by Luckie Yasukochi

A delicate watercolor fabric serves as the background for a symmetrical four star design in this elegant variation. Shades of lavender and pink alternate with rich jewel tones to create the center stars. *See instructions on page 82.*

Royal Star
Twenty-five Block Quilt
by Teresa Varnes

Teresa's contemporary quilt design features a
large center star in a jade fabric, set off by
floral triangles with tones of mauve. The
verdant center is echoed in a thin border, then
finished with the floral fabric. *See instructions
on page 90.*

Water Lily
Twenty-five Block Quilt
by Patricia Knoechel and Susan Sells

Computers bring quilting to a new frontier of
creativity – this enchanting quilt was team
designed using an illustrator program. Seven
variant shades were used to create this beauti-
ful and intricate picture quilt. *See instructions
on page 92.*

50" x 50"

Through the Looking Glass
Twenty-five Block Quilt
by Sue Bouchard

Sue used three fabrics in a one block repeat to create a simple and striking design. This distinctive quilt illustrates a different look for the Kaleidoscope pattern in purple, sea green and cream.

One Block Repeat Quilt

Make the total number of blocks for the quilt from Star/Background blocks. Combine 5" Star Center strips with 5" Background strips for the total number of 5" Background strips. Purchase an additional fabric for the 4" strips for Corner Triangles.

Three Fabrics
■ Background - 1 yd
   (6) 5" strips

■ Star - 1½ yds
   (6) 5" strips

Second Border
   (5) 4½" strips

Batting
   57" square

■ Corner Triangles - 1½ yds
   (5) 4" strips
      (50) 4" squares, then cut on diagonal

First Border
   (5) 2" strips

Binding
   (6) 3" strips

Backing
   3⅓ yds
      2 equal pieces

Layer strips right sides together.
Cut triangles and sew these pairs:

 100 pairs - 6 strips of each

Sew Pairs into Blocks
Block ① Make 25

Add Corner Triangles

100 pieces

87

Orion and Seven Sisters
Thirty-five Block Quilt by Eleanor Burns

Multi-colored stars of burgundy, mauve, powder blue, and green florals dance across a quilted ivory background. Designed and created by Eleanor Burns, and machine quilted by Deborah Steidley.

52" x 68"

Select the size quilt you want to make, and count the stars. For each Star and Center, coordinate different fabrics with the same Background fabric. Refer to your particular size quilt for Background yardage.

For each Star, you need…
 (2) 5" x 11" Star strips
 (1) 5" x 11" Center strip
 (1) 5" x 11" Background strip

These strips are enough for one Star/Center block, and one Star/Background block. Repeat for each star in quilt.

Layer Strips Right Sides Together.
Cut Triangles and Sew these Pairs:

Sew Star/Center block.   Leave Star/Background in pairs.

  4 pairs - 1 strip of each   Star on Center

4 pairs - 1 strip of each   Star on Background

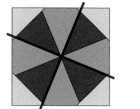

Repeat this step for all stars in quilts.

Planning the Quilt

Lay out the Star/Center blocks, leaving space between the blocks for the Star/Background pairs. Place Star/Background pairs with the same Star fabric around each Star/Center block, forming points on each star.

Once a Star/Background block is complete with four pairs, slip the block onto the Square Up ruler. Carry it to your sewing area, and sew together with Corner Triangles.

Finish quilt with Edge Blocks, following the directions for your particular size quilt.

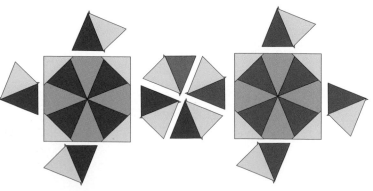

Prairie Sunburst, *see color photo page 85*

Five Fabrics

Cut strips selvage to selvage.

☐ Fabric 1 - ½ yd
   (2) 5" strips
   (1) 4" strip
     (10) 4" squares, then cut on diagonal

■ Fabric 2 - 1½ yds
   (2) 5" strips
   (1) 4" strip
     (4) 4" squares, then cut on diagonal
  Second Border
   (5) 4" strips
  Binding
   (5) 3" strips

  Backing - 1¼ yds
  Batting - 40" square

■ Fabric 3 - ½ yd
   (1) 5" strip
  First Border
   (4) 2" strips

■ Fabric 4 - ¼ yd
   (1) 5" strip

■ Fabric 5 - ¾ yd
   (1) 5" strip
   (1) 4" strip
     (4) 4" squares, then cut on diagonal

Layer strips right sides together.
Cut triangles and sew these pairs:

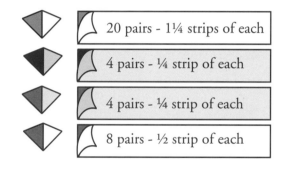

20 pairs - 1¼ strips of each
4 pairs - ¼ strip of each
4 pairs - ¼ strip of each
8 pairs - ½ strip of each

Sew Pairs into Blocks

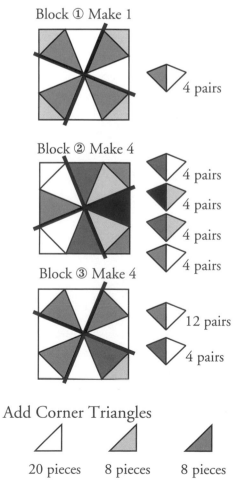

Block ① Make 1
  4 pairs

Block ② Make 4
  4 pairs
  4 pairs
  4 pairs
  4 pairs

Block ③ Make 4
  12 pairs
  4 pairs

Add Corner Triangles

20 pieces   8 pieces   8 pieces

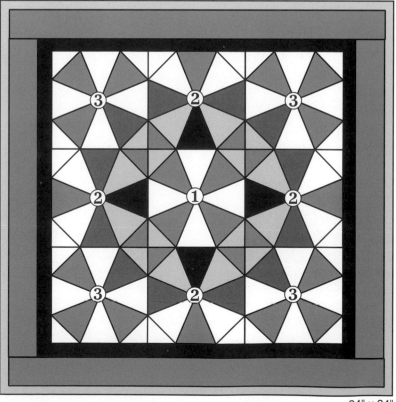

34" x 34"

Royal Star, *see color photo page 86*

Four Fabrics

Cut strips selvage to selvage.

- ■ Fabric 1 - ½ yd
  - (1) 5" strip
  - First Border
  - (4) 2" strips
- ■ Fabric 2 - 1⅔ yds
  - (2) 5" strips
  - (1) 4" strip
    - (8) 4" squares, then cut on diagonal
  - Second Border
  - (5) 4" strips
  - Binding
  - (5) 3" strips
- ■ Fabric 3 - 1 yd
  - (5) 5" strips
  - (1) 4" strip
    - (10) 4" squares, then cut on diagonal
- □ Fabric 4 - 1¼ yds
  - (5) 5" strips
  - (4) 4" strips
    - (32) 4" squares, then cut on diagonal

Backing - 3 yds
  - (2) equal pieces
Batting - 54" square

Layer strips right sides together.
Cut triangles and sew these pairs:

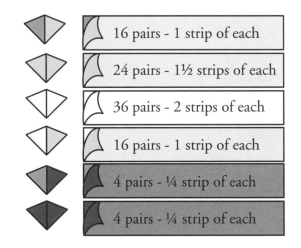

16 pairs - 1 strip of each

24 pairs - 1½ strips of each

36 pairs - 2 strips of each

16 pairs - 1 strip of each

4 pairs - ¼ strip of each

4 pairs - ¼ strip of each

Sew Pairs into Blocks

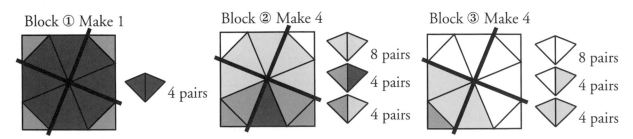

Block ① Make 1
4 pairs

Block ② Make 4
8 pairs
4 pairs
4 pairs

Block ③ Make 4
8 pairs
4 pairs
4 pairs

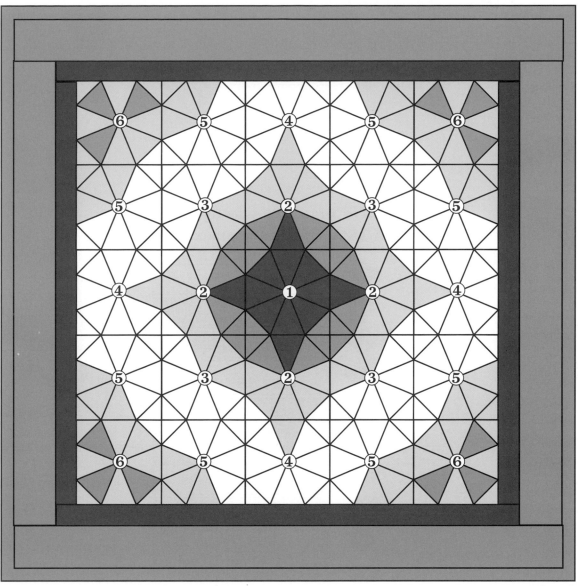

50" x 50"

Block ④ Make 4

12 pairs

4 pairs

Block ⑤ Make 8

8 pairs

16 pairs

8 pairs

Block ⑥ Make 4

12 pairs

4 pairs

Add Corner Pieces   20 Pieces   64 Pieces   16 Pieces

Water Lily Variation, *see color photo page 86*

Seven Fabrics

Cut strips selvage to selvage.

■ Fabric 1 - (Green) ½ yd
   (3) 5" strips

■ Fabric 2 - (Dark Pink) ⅓ yd
   (2) 5" strips

■ Fabric 3 - (Medium Pink) ⅝ yd
   (2) 5" strips
   (2) 4" strips
      (20) 4" squares, then cut on diagonal

■ Fabric 4 - (Dark Blue) ½ yd
   (2) 5" strips
   (1) 4" strip
      (4) 4" squares, then cut on diagonal

■ Fabric 5 - (Medium Blue) ⅜ yd
   (1) 5" strip
   Folded Border
   (5) 1¼" strips

■ Fabric 6 - (Light Blue) 2 yds
   (3) 5" strips
   (3) 4" strips
      (26) 4" squares, then cut on diagonal
   Second Border
   (5) 4½" strips
   Binding
   (5) 3" strips

□ Fabric 7 - ⅔ yd
   (2) 5" strips
   First Border
   (4) 2½" strips

Backing - 3 yds
Batting - 56" square

Layer strips right sides together.
Cut triangles and sew these pairs:

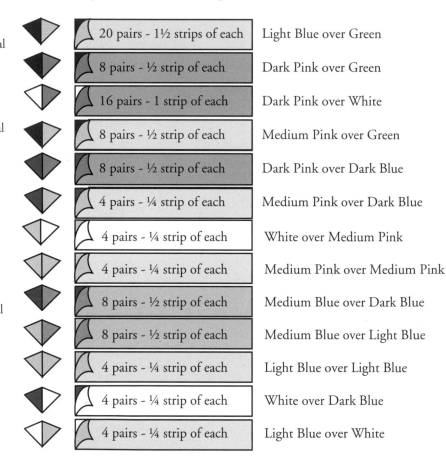

20 pairs - 1½ strips of each	Light Blue over Green
8 pairs - ½ strip of each	Dark Pink over Green
16 pairs - 1 strip of each	Dark Pink over White
8 pairs - ½ strip of each	Medium Pink over Green
8 pairs - ½ strip of each	Dark Pink over Dark Blue
4 pairs - ¼ strip of each	Medium Pink over Dark Blue
4 pairs - ¼ strip of each	White over Medium Pink
4 pairs - ¼ strip of each	Medium Pink over Medium Pink
8 pairs - ½ strip of each	Medium Blue over Dark Blue
8 pairs - ½ strip of each	Medium Blue over Light Blue
4 pairs - ¼ strip of each	Light Blue over Light Blue
4 pairs - ¼ strip of each	White over Dark Blue
4 pairs - ¼ strip of each	Light Blue over White

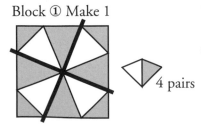

Block ① Make 1

4 pairs

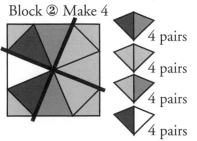

Block ② Make 4

4 pairs
4 pairs
4 pairs
4 pairs

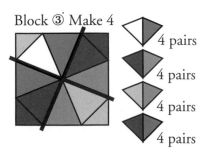

Block ③ Make 4

4 pairs
4 pairs
4 pairs
4 pairs

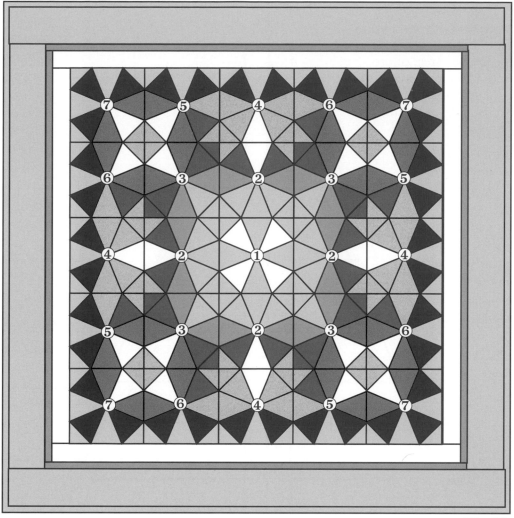

52" x 52"

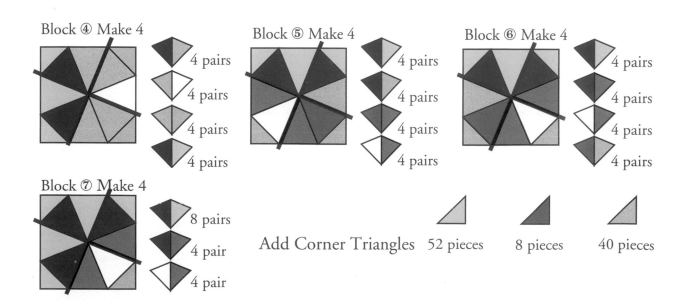

Block ④ Make 4

4 pairs
4 pairs
4 pairs
4 pairs

Block ⑤ Make 4

4 pairs
4 pairs
4 pairs
4 pairs

Block ⑥ Make 4

4 pairs
4 pairs
4 pairs
4 pairs

Block ⑦ Make 4

8 pairs
4 pair
4 pair

Add Corner Triangles   52 pieces   8 pieces   40 pieces

93

Kaleidoscope Ruler Template

Use a plexiglass ruler with these same angles and lines. If a ruler of this type is not available in your area, photo copy this one and glue to heavy cardboard. Trace the triangle shape onto your strip sets. Rotary cut on the lines with a 6" x 12" ruler.

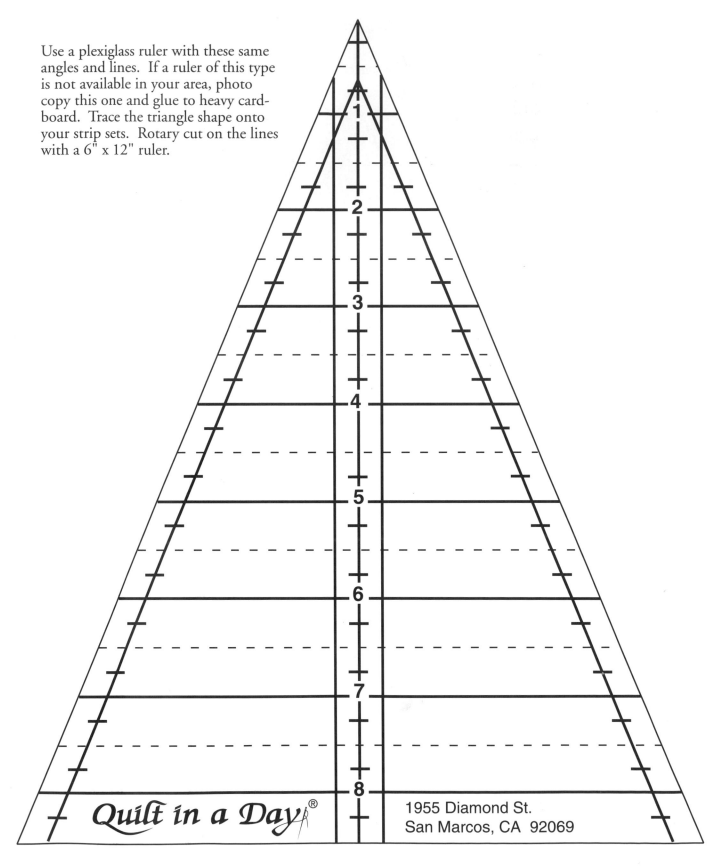

Quilt in a Day®

1955 Diamond St.
San Marcos, CA 92069

You can order Quilt in a Day's Kaleidoscope ruler by calling 1-800-777-4852.

Acknowledgements

A grateful thank you to my students who tested the instructions.

My sincere appreciation to the QIAD quiltmakers for their "works of art."

And a special thanks to Carla Wellendorf for her generous assistance in researching the Kaleidoscope block.

Index

Order Information

Quilt in a Day books offer a wide range of techniques and are directed toward a variety of skill levels. If you do not have a quilt shop in your area, you may write for a complete catalog and current price list of all books and patterns published by Quilt in a Day®, Inc., 1955 Diamond Street, San Marcos, CA 92069 or call to order toll free 1 800 777-4852 between the hours of 8am – 5pm Pacific Time.

Easy

These books are easy enough for beginners of any age.
Log Cabin Quilt in a Day
Irish Chain Quilt
Bits & Pieces Quilt
Trip Around the World Quilt
Heart's Delight Wallhanging
Scrap Quilt
Rail Fence Quilt
Dresden Placemats
Flying Geese Quilt
Star for all Seasons Placemats
Winning Hand Quilt
Courthouse Steps Quilt
From Blocks to Quilt

Applique

While these books offer a variety of techniques, easy applique is featured in each.
Applique in a Day
Dresden Plate Quilt
Sunbonnet Sue Visits Quilt in a Day
Recycled Treasures
Country Cottages and More
Creating with Color
Spools & Tools Wallhanging
Dutch Windmills Quilt

Intermediate to Advanced

With a little Quilt in a Day experience, these books offer a rewarding project.
Trio of Treasured Quilts
Lover's Knot Quilt
Amish Quilt
May Basket Quilt
Morning Star Quilt
Friendship Quilt
Tulip Quilt

Star Log Cabin Quilt
Burgoyne Surrounded Quilt
Bird's Eye Quilt
Snowball Quilt
Tulip Table Runner

Holiday

When a favorite holiday is approaching, Quilt in a Day is there to help you plan.
Christmas Quilts and Crafts
Country Christmas
Bunnies & Blossoms
Patchwork Santa
Last Minute Gifts
Angel of Antiquity
Log Cabin Wreath Wallhanging
Log Cabin Tree Wallhanging
Country Flag Wallhanging
Lover's Knot Placemats

Sampler

Always and forever popular are books with a variety of patterns.
The Sampler
Block Party Series 1, Quilter's Year
Block Party Series 2, Baskets and Flowers
Block Party Series 3, Quilters' Almanac
Block Party Series 4, Christmas Traditions
Block Party Series 5, Pioneer Sampler

Angle Piecing

Quilt in a Day "template free" methods make angle cutting less of a challenge.
Diamond Log Cabin Tablecloth or Treeskirt
Pineapple Quilt
Blazing Star Tablecloth
Schoolhouse Quilt
Radiant Star Quilt